APACHE

WRITTEN AND ILLUSTRATED BY

LAND

ROSS SANTEE

UNIVERSITY OF NEBRASKA PRESS • LINCOLN

International Standard Book Number 0–8032–5737–6

Library of Congress Catalog Card Number 47–11035

First Bison Book printing: May 1971
Most recent printing shown by first digit below:

4   5   6   7   8   9   10

Bison Book edition reproduced from the first edition
by arrangement with Charles Scribner's Sons.

FOREWORD

THIS started out to be a book of sketches with a little text and the thing got out of hand. It would be impossible to list all the friends who helped me in this chore since it began when I first started making sketches of the Apaches and rode the range with some of them, many years ago.

At that time the idea of a book of sketches never occurred to me. I have always liked to draw. Wet-nursing a bunch of saddle horses gave me much time to mess around. To help pass the time I was forever sketching everything in sight—the hills, the horses, the Apaches, the punchers. In camp I was always a good listener but it was years later before I ever tried to put any stories down.

It was my privilege, as editor of "Arizona, A State Guide," to have every word of research, and there were millions of them, pass before my eye. And knowing my weakness for the Apaches, there was much my friends dug up for me.

Mulford Winsor made much of the research possible, and gracious Mrs. Good could always put her hands on anything we wanted. A bow to Mrs. Edith Kitt of Tucson. Frances Sanitas, Joe Miller and Leslie Gregory were forever finding bits that would have otherwise been lost. And Johnnie, better known as Raymond Carlson, editor of "Arizona Highways," was forever steering me up little trails I would otherwise have missed.

The old Territorial newspapers, the Arizona and New Mexico Historical Reviews were combed, all of Farish's "Arizona History" and everything Dr. Frank Lockwood, that gentleman and historian of the University of Arizona, ever put in print. To list the books read would be impossible, too, but I will pass along a few, offhand, that meant most to me.

Pattie's Diary, published in 1831, gives a picture of the trappers in Arizona as early as 1825. "Life Among the Apaches," San Francisco, 1868, by John C. Cremony, gives one pictures of the Apache and his relation to the American. Cremony was with Bartlett when he made the U. S. and Mexican Boundary Survey in 1851. Later, as an officer in the California Column, he was in the fight at Apache Pass.

"Adventures in Apache Land," by J. Ross Browne, has been read many, many times. An artist as well as writer, Browne sketched with a shotgun in his lap. Always a keen observer, he left a fine pictorial record. Unlike so many, nowadays, who rush into print with an adventure story after a glance at a coyote from a passing car, Browne never took his adventures too seriously and always wrote with quiet humor.

I think "The Apache Indians" is Dr. Lockwood's outstanding book and I liked "Apache" by Will Levington Comfort, and "Death in the Desert" by Paul Wellman. "Apache Agent," by Woolworth Clum, is the story of his father, John P. Clum, Indian Agent at San Carlos. While young Agent Clum had the knack of picking capable men to work with him, he gives them casual mention.

I liked the salty Britton Davis who pulls no punches in "The Truth About Geronimo." However, to my mind all are shaded—with the exception of J. Ross Browne—by that modest and gallant soldier, Captain John G. Bourke. While "On the Border With Crook," Scribner's, 1896, is the only book I'll list, everything that Bourke wrote is worth reading. Bourke not only knew the Apaches, he wrote as poets should.

Charlie Clark told me the story of "Brother Tom." "Two-Bits" came from Arthur Ensign. Judge Wentworth in Globe was the only man I found who had ever known Felix Knox. Ethel Larsen was responsible for "Man of Peace," David Harer was her great-grandfather. "The White Man's Way" came from John P. Clum's stories of his Apache friend in the Arizona Historical Review. Years ago an old cowpuncher, whose name I have forgotten, told me the Sieber story when we were working at the Bar F Bar outfit together. I had many old friends who knew the "Apache Kid."

I knew old "Burro Frenchy" and often drank his wine. In "Blood Brothers" I went to Lockwood and Farish for the story of Tom Jeffords and Cochise. Nor did I at any time attempt to throw history around. While I don't think the actual conversation between Tom Jeffords and Cochise was as stilted as it sounds, I took no liberties. I tried to put Uncle Jimmie Stevens' stories down just as they were told.

They say it is customary to dedicate a book, so this little one is dedicated to an old Apache friend, gone these many years, who had all the virtues of his race and enough of its vices to make him lovable.

To Old Jim Whitehead of blessed memory.

CONTENTS

CONTENTS

APACHE LAND

I

WHEN the ponies quieted down in the morning it was the custom for the horse-wrangler to go to camp and auger the cook for a spell. If the cook was in good humor, the wrangler might be invited to drink coffee and help himself to the cold steak. This, however, was always the exception and never the rule.

On this particular morning I met a young Apache friend, a boy of about twelve years, known only as Johnnie Coo. Johnnie wouldn't weigh eighty pounds soaking wet but he was as active and quick as a cat. Unlike so many of the Apache children who looked at us from a mask, Johnnie Coo always had a warm smile for any cowpuncher who passed and his dark eyes were as bright as a squirrel's.

He was trying to supplement the family meat larder; when I rode up he was busy with a long stick at a wood rat's nest. Johnnie liked Bull Durham cigarettes and he liked chewing tobacco. As usual he eyed me expectantly and when, instead of tobacco, I offered him a stirrup he climbed aboard—after tying two dead wood rats to a string.

Old Slick an' Greasy, the cook, was busy with his pots and pans. He looked our layout over with a jaundiced eye, then went on about his work, ignoring us completely. After all, a horse-wrangler, an Apache boy—with two dead wood rats—riding to his fire was nothing to cheer about. But I knew Old Slick an' Greasy was not as tough and hardboiled as he would have others believe, so I said nothing. Presently, Old Slick looked up as if he had just discovered us. "Git down," he said, "you an' yore gut-eatin' friend; the coffee's hot an' there's cold steak in the oven—but don't bring them dead rats into camp."

We dismounted and what my young Apache friend ate that morning, I think is worth recording. Johnnie Coo put away six small steaks that were not as small as they might have been. The only reason he didn't have a higher score was the fact that the meat played out. There were some frijole beans left in the pot, and when Old Slick gave me the "go" sign, I passed my friend a plate and spoon. Johnnie ate four plates of beans and the pot was clean; he ate eight large biscuits as well, washing them down with several cups of coffee.

Old Slick had stopped his work and was watching Johnnie in amazement. But it was not until Johnnie had cleaned the camp that the cook said: "Git him out of here before he starts eatin' on the pack-saddle riggin' or a latigo."

It was thirty years ago. To me, Apaches and cowpunchers will always be associated together, for in those days the big outfits, the white outfits, ran their cattle on both the upper and lower Apache reservations in Arizona. Some of the white outfits on the reservation used a few Apache cowboys during the roundup, spring and fall, and there was an occasional Apache cowboy who worked the year 'round as a regular hand.

Many Apache cowboys brought their families and often their relatives to the roundup. They set up their wickiups some distance from our camp but they were always on hand to carry off the guts when the outfit killed a beef. They seemed to be always hungry.

One evening we had just butchered; as usual, we had hung the beef in a tree to cool for the night. The Apaches were carrying off the guts when we heard a ruckus. Two old Apache bucks, their matted hair streaked with gray, had drawn their knives and were snarling at each other over the paunch much as two ranch dogs will face each other over a bone, each afraid to pick it up, knowing that if he does he will start hostilities.

"Let 'em fight," said a puncher. "Hell, yes," said another, "let 'em kill each other." But the foreman intervened. The two old Indians divided the paunch and put up their knives. To the disappointment of some of the punchers, there was no fight.

Some of the Apache cowboys were undernourished when they came

to the roundup. But after a few weeks' diet of beef, frijole beans and biscuits, their dark skin glowed in the sun like a piece of bacon rind.

Meat that had soured or was tainted, that would have made a white puncher deathly sick, apparently did not affect the Apaches. One night two quarters of beef, hung out to cool, were rained on and soured. The foreman gave both quarters to our camp followers, who put on a feed next day that lasted far into the night. Men, women and children gorged themselves on sour meat until they were as full as ticks, without any ill effects. For my money, the Apache of thirty years ago is still champion when it comes to stowing his vittles away in quantities, depending, of course, on when he could get them.

Lean and hungry Apache dogs, some as big as loafer wolves, were always present. They served a twofold purpose: at night they supplemented the bedding in the tepee and they often pulled down calves on the range for their Apache masters. The Indian dogs hated the smell of a white man and the ranch dogs had the same aversion to an Indian.

For the most part the Apaches always knew where the punchers were riding. A smoke signal would go up on a distant peak; they also used the sun and mirror to signal each other and they had other means of communication, too. They knew who every white puncher was who rode the range. On Mescal one day I spotted a buck who was off the Reservation. At sight of the rider he quit his horse and climbed a tree. "Ketchum acorn," said the Apache. "You ketchum beef!" "No likum beef," said the Apache; "ketchum acorn."

"Come on down," I said, "an' let's see your pass." The Apache had no pass. "Want me to take you to San Carlos?" "You no take me to San Carlos," said the Apache. "What makes you think so?" "You friend." "You don't even know who I am." "You Slim," said the Apache, "you friend." I had never seen the Indian before to my knowledge but without further ado he told me the color and the brand on every horse that was in my mount.

The outfit expected the Apaches to kill a beef any time they could get away with it, and punchers, riding the range, often found plenty of evidence. But catching an Indian in the act was something else again. The Old Man and I were riding Tanks Canyon together when we spotted horse tracks that had no business there. Two Apache riders had been running a yearling the day before. The sign showed where the yearling had been roped, then one Apache led while the other followed, apparently working on the critter's rump with the double of his rope. The ground was soft and the trail was easy to follow until they got into the rock tanks.

We cut sign but we could not work it out. We had dismounted for a smoke when, by accident, I saw what had happened to the yearling. Under a jetting rock was what had been inside the paunch. Later we found where they had butchered, that was all. The two Apaches and the yearling they'd killed had disappeared into thin air.

Jimmie Gibson and I were riding a trail together on the upper range when Jimmie pulled his pony up. As I followed his gaze I saw two small branches, broken and hanging about a foot from the tip; they could only have been broken by someone on horseback. As Jimmie's eyes went to the ground, I saw the two crossed sticks directly below them. One stick lay along the trail but the other pointed up a side canyon. "Come on,"

said Jimmie, "we may find something." We had not ridden a hundred
yards up the side canyon until we found two quarters of beef hung in a
cedar. Apaches riding down the trail had left it for friends who were
following. "It's probably a Cross S beef," said Jimmie. "They think
we're so doggone stupid we should take it anyway, even if it is partly
soured." But we didn't.

According to the white man's standards, the Apaches were not good

cowboys. As a matter of fact, the only thing they did better than a white
cowpuncher was trail. The only Apache I ever knew who held his own
with the white cowboys was Jim Whitehead. Jim was not a bucking-
horse rider but with wild cattle Jim took nothing from his white brother.
Old Jim could follow a trail that was a closed book to most white
punchers. We often hunted horses together. After Jim had showed me
a pebble moved or a bruised blade of grass, and told me how long since

it had been back in place, it was all perfectly obvious. But Old Jim finally gave up on me as ever being a good trailer.

It was hard for me to accept the fact that the Apache, wildest, cruelest and most feared of all Indians—the last to "come in"—was a timid person. But he was. The white cowpunchers would dab their lines on anything that moved, no matter how wild and big the steer or how rough the country; and some of them rode horses when they did it that an Apache would not even approach in the corral.

But once an Apache rode a horse, it was seldom the pony ever got

his head up again. It was the Apache's custom to tie up a wild one he had caught and give him no feed or water for several days. Then the Indian would lead the pony to the creek and let him drink his fill. With a paunch full of water and in deep sand, halfway to the pony's knees, the Apache would saddle him and crawl aboard.

There was a blue pony at the Cross S outfit that was always in the rough string and he was really hard to ride. Just let some little thing go wrong and the blue pony would break in two and go to pitching. Nor did the peelers protest when the Old Man finally trade him off to an Indian. It was less than a month later, when the outfit was eating dinner at the lower ranch, that a squaw rode into the water corral. It was the blue she rode but rather the worse for wear. Aside from the kids she carried behind her, the squaw carried part of the family belongings as well. The rough-string riders took their ribbing. One could not but feel sorry for the horse, even an outlaw horse must have something in his paunch to keep him pitching.

In camp the Apaches kept pretty much to themselves. They always made their beds a little way from ours. If the weather was good we rolled our beds on the ground and slept in the open. The Apaches always tried to bed down under some kind of shelter, even if it was only a few bushes. It was always warmer that way when bedding was short and I came to like their little fires, too, where each Apache squatted over his own fire and warmed himself without having half the carcass burn.

When an Apache went hunting he didn't go weighed down with equipment. Nor was the ammunition he carried any strain upon a horse. Compared to a dude, the cowboy travels light and when he has to, the puncher will travel as light as any Indian. But the Apache hunter always travels that way. If he didn't happen to have a blanket or quilt, the Apache slept in his saddle blankets, which might be a couple of gunny sacks. First he built a fire on the ground, then when the ground was warm, he raked the coals away, curled up with his feet to the hot coals and went to sleep.

The Apache usually carried two tin cans, one for coffee and the other to boil his meat in. He carried a little flat tin that weighed only a few ounces to cook his bread on. A little flour in a sack, a little salt, coffee and sugar, sometimes—that was all.

Old Archie stopped at the lower ranch one day on his way to the high country for a hunt. He carried the above equipment, the only extra Archie had was a little dog he called Ten Cents. This half-pint mongrel pooch and Old Archie were inseparable. Old Archie ate a meal at the ranch, a real bait, too. Still he hung around. We finally got it out of him that while he was going on a hunt he had no ammunition, so one of the boys gave him six .30-30 shells. "Goin' to kill a deer, Archie?" said a puncher who happened along as Old Archie was fondling the shells. "Kill turkey, too," said Archie. With those six .30-30 shells the old Indian killed four deer and two wild turkeys in the month that he was gone.

The Apaches wore moccasins when they hunted. Since ammunition was expensive and hard to get, none was ever wasted. Old Archie would stalk a deer all day. If there was the slightest chance of missing, Old Archie wouldn't shoot. In his moccasins the old Indian made no sound. Often he would approach from nowhere. First thing we knew the old

Indian would be standing not ten feet away nor had we seen or heard him. It was Old Archie's idea of a joke; it was disconcerting, too.

Herding horses on the mountain one bright fall day, it was just by chance I glimpsed my friend, Archie, slipping toward me through the cedars. I was dismounted at the time, holding my pony by the bridle reins. As far as Old Archie could observe I was watching some saddle horses that were starting to move down the mesa. But from the tail of my eye I was watching the old Indian as he slipped silently toward me, taking advantage of each bit of cover. Old Archie was still a good fifty feet away when I jerked my six-shooter and wheeled his way.

"Cha—Cha—" yelled Archie, dropping his .30-30 and holding both hands high. "It's Archie—friend." "You scared me, Archie." I put up the gun and handed him my tobacco sack. Old Archie was upset, his old hands still trembled as he built a cigarette. As long as he lived Old Archie never tried to slip up on me again.

Most of the white punchers either tolerated the Indians or treated

them with open contempt. And we were resented by the Apaches. It never flared into the open as the Apaches well knew that the cowpuncher is easily provoked to violence. But the Apaches' resentment was always there—an averted face as we rode by a wickiup, in little things that were easier felt than seen. And we were intruders.

After all, it was their land and their reservation, deeded to them in solemn treaty by our government. The white outfits paid a grazing fee— so much per head; the fee varied over the years. I have forgotten the exact figures but it was not much over a dollar a head. A counter, usually a white man, represented the Indians during the roundup. One year eight thousand head were counted at the Cross S outfit and the owners had a wall-eyed fit. Yet they knew that less than half the cattle had been tallied. The Cross S outfit was a small outfit, too, when compared with the "Cherries" or Chiricahua Cattle Company, and the Double Circles. If the Apaches benefited in any way, it was not obvious. The grazing fees went for administration purposes.

Some of the Apaches were my friends and I was often invited to their wickiups. This, of course, was beneath the dignity of most cowpunchers; but, after all, the relationship of the horse-wrangler to the top hand was not unlike that of a buck private to a top sergeant.

The wickiup as a dwelling has many advantages. Built by the squaws from the materials at hand, poles of pine, juniper or mesquite were placed in a circle and set a few inches in the ground. The tops are securely lashed, completing a conical framework. This is covered with grass or brush and over all are lashed pieces of canvas, often a skirt or other wearing apparel. It could be built in a few hours and abandoned or burned without regret. If it is for a short stay, it is small, while some of the permanent wickiups are large and roomy affairs. A ramada made of poles set in the ground and covered with brush is often added.

On the upper or White River Reservation a little vestibule of wood and a tight door is usually found. Tightly covered, the wickiup is snug, too, even in the coldest weather. In warm weather the sides are raised, allowing the occupants to catch the breeze. It is said that the wickiup is often an indication of the character of the builder: if it is large and roomy, the squaw is more inclined to give good tulapai parties and be generous; if the tepee is small, the builder is apt to be stingy.

In good weather the cooking is done outside. In bad weather it is done in the tepee. The smoke, or at least some of it, goes up through the vent or smoke hole. During the day the bedding—quilts, blankets, etc.—is either piled against the walls or hung outside on the bushes to air. The cooking, of course, is done on an open fire; utensils come from the trader's store and there is always the Dutch oven. The five gallon oil can was standard, too, even thirty years ago.

A piece of tarp was usually spread and the family sat on the ground when they ate, much after the manner of their white brothers and sisters at a picnic. If plates and spoons were short, the individuals ate from a common dish using their fingers. Meat—when they could get it—was the favorite food, eaten fresh, roasted or boiled. Stew with vegetables was a common dish; corn was often roasted with the husks in the hot embers. In hot weather some of the meat was "jerked." Cut in thin strips, it was hung outside on the jerky line; when dry it would keep indefinitely. Pounded into small bits, it was often cooked in gravy with hominy, onions or chile.

Corn was used in many ways; after grinding it on the metate or grind-

ing stone, it was mixed into a stiff batter and poured into the Dutch oven and browned on both sides in a little grease. The lid was then placed on the oven, hot coals were placed on the lid and it was baked over a slow fire. The tortilla was their favorite bread as well as mine. Made from corn meal ground on the metate, the cakes were rolled, often paper thin, and baked over a large piece of tin or in the frying pan.

Pork was taboo, but of late years it is eaten. Only recently I sat on a stool at a restaurant in White River beside "Chicken," one of the old Apache scouts, and we both relished a bait of pork chops. Fish was also taboo as was anything that ate fish. An old cowpuncher who had lived for years among the Apaches once told me the custom originated after a great drouth. The game had left the country and the Indians were living on trout. At the same time an epidemic of smallpox occurred and the medicine man, always a resourceful person, said it was simply the spots on the trout coming out.

In addition to their patches of corn, beans, pumpkins, squash and melons, the Apaches gathered a variety of wild foods: acorns, piñon nuts, walnuts, juniper berries, roots and seeds, mesquite beans. They gathered wild onions, wild potatoes and the fruit of the prickly pear and the saguaro cactus. Mescal cooked in great pits was a favorite dish. Tea was made from a certain bush, white punchers used it, too; the punchers simply spoke of the bush as the "tea store" or tea bush.

Wood rats were considered a delicacy; in this I was perfectly willing to take them at their word. Strung together on a string, the dead rats

were lowered into a can of boiling water. Since the Apaches never bothered to clean or skin the rats, they looked far from appetizing when
cooked and ready to be eaten.

Nothing was ever wasted when a beef was killed and the guts were in
great favor. This was something I came to really enjoy when I knew they
had been thoroughly cleaned. Often I sat outside his wickiup and talked

far into the night with Old Jim Whitehead, friend of blessed memory,
and as we talked, Old Jim and I, each with a green stick in hand broiled
small pieces of guts over the hot coals. Often at a meal with my Apache
friends I did not know what I was eating. If I disliked the taste, I simply
passed but I never did ask questions.

Unfortunately, not all my Apache friends were as clean as Old Jim
and his family. One night when Jim and I were in cow camp together an
Apache rode in who had no bedding. Nor did Old Jim offer to share his

bed or split his blankets. The Apache had curled up by the fire to sleep.
Old Jim said nothing when I gave the Indian a couple of my blankets.
But next morning when our guest had departed Old Jim took my two
blankets and threw them over a big ant hill. In speaking of our overnight
guest, Jim said: "Him lousy like what you call pet coon; ants eat lice, ants
eat nits, too."

It was a common sight as we rode past a wickiup to see squaws and
children picking lice from each other's hair. Short hair and even a bald
head are sometimes an advantage.

Sometime in the seventies, the Apache woman adopted a style of
white woman's dress that has come on down through the years. The skirts
are voluminous affairs of eighteen or twenty yards of the brightest print
obtainable. In color they are orange, scarlet, blue or green, with a deep
flounce and many rows of ornamental braid. A blouse hangs to the hips
from a smooth yoke, high-necked, full sleeves and never belted. Her long
black hair hangs loose, often with bangs and bobbed at the shoulders. Nor
did she pinch her feet in shoes. Moccasins of buckskin, that were leggings
as well, were usually rolled below the knee and soled with rawhide with
a protruding tip. Little Apache girls, just able to toddle, are often
dressed exactly as their mothers.

Beady-eyed babies, sewed into canopied cradle-boards, were ever
present. The carrying strap was often over the shoulders but more often
it was across the mother's forehead. Youngsters out of the cradle-board
were slung in pieces of cloth and carried on the mother's back. If a widow,
the squaw wore a cape, often of a different color from her dress. A few
old crones still wore a tight skirt that hung to the knees, and little else.
Often the skirt was made of buckskin. On rare occasions one saw an old
woman with the end of her nose cut off, a squaw who had been unfaithful.

Aside from building the wickiup, carrying wood and water, cooking,
irrigating or working a garden patch, the women dressed buckskin, made
trays and baskets. Of simple design, to me the burden basket trimmed
with buckskin was especially beautiful. And there was the tus or water
jar lined with pitch. Unlike the Navajos, the Apaches make no rugs or
jewelry. Yet Navajo and Mexican blankets were not uncommon in a
tepee. Some Navajo jewelry was seen, but after the five and ten cent store
opened in Globe, Mr. Woolworth's jewelry was much in evidence.

The Apache women have small hands and feet. In spite of the work they did they were inclined to stoutness yet they were not unattractive. The men, for the most part, wore cowboy clothes, blue cotton shirts and levis (copper-riveted overalls); yet for a shindig bright-colored shirts appeared. Many wore a bright scarf knotted tight about the neck like a Hollywood cowboy, though never worn by the working cowpuncher in Arizona. The big hat was standard.

When Old Jim and I were driving some saddle horses from the horse camp to the lower ranch we found a hat along the road. It had evidently blown from a passing car and not been missed. Since the hat was new and it was a good one, a 3X Stetson Beaver, it looked for a time as if the hat might go to me, as the back of Old Jim's head was flat from being strapped to a cradle-board as a baby. But Old Jim was always resourceful, he simply put the Stetson on sideways and wore the hat that way.

The working of the Apache cowboy's mind was often hard to follow. The foreman sent an Apache with a note to one of the line camps, telling Dick to come in to the home ranch next day, they were making a small gather and he would be needed. It was two weeks before Dick showed up at the ranch, then he came in after a packload of chuck. "Didn't you get my note a couple of weeks ago?" said the foreman. "Hell, no," said Dick, "I never got any note."

The foreman called the Apache. "I thought I told you to go to Dick's camp and give him the note; if he wasn't there, I told you to leave the note in his camp." "Me go Dick's camp," said the Apache. "Dick gone but me leave note like you tell." "Well, where did you leave the note? He never got it." "Me leave note under big rock outside Dick's camp. Wind she blow hard in Dick's camp; me leave note under big rock so note no blow away." Back in his line camp Dick found the note just where the Apache said he put it, safely hidden under a big rock. The note was safe, it hadn't blown away.

As a usual thing an Apache spoke the truth, but it occasionally had strange ramifications. Shorty was on his way to town from the Flying H's when an Apache, known as Indian George, caught up with him. "Long time my friend," said George as he pulled his horse alongside, "you no talk, me no talk." Shorty recognized some kind of build-up but he didn't know what it was about. "What do you want?" said Shorty. "Whiskey," replied Indian George. "You know Indians ain't allowed to drink, it would get us both in trouble."

"Long time my friend," said the Indian, "you no talk, me no talk."
They had often worked together. Shorty liked George who finally broke
him down. There was a hog ranch a few miles from town where whiskey
and women could be had. Shorty agreed to buy the Indian a half pint. He
promised to leave it by a certain large rock along the trail. "Long time
my friend," said Indian George to Shorty as they parted, "you no talk,
me no talk."

It so happened that some officers were on the watch that day for
bootleggers peddling whiskey to the Indians. They knew Shorty was not
a bootlegger; when they saw him leave the hog ranch and stop for a
moment at the big rock they thought nothing of it. But when the Indian
rode up and stopped a little later they became suspicious. Indian George
had dismounted, uncorked his bottle and was spreading his feet to brace
himself for a long drink when the officers rode up. "Where'd you get the
whiskey, Indian?" "Find um under rock," said the Apache. "Well, who
put it there?" "Shorty, I guess," said the Apache.

The Apache has a keen sense of humor. Among themselves or with
a white friend they laugh and joke a lot. When the spirit moves him, a
buck will whip his squaw; in a fit of temper he may even kill her, for
the Apache is still given to flaming fits of rage and savage temper. Yet
I never saw an Apache, man or woman, strike or punish a child. Little
girls were usually at their mother's heels and played with home made
dolls. The boys played with small bows and arrows; hunted wood rats,
cotton-tails, jack rabbits, quail and squirrels. Like ranchers' children they
were on a horse long before they could walk. They were always in the

open and in spite of what they ate—often, what they didn't—most of
them were active and healthy. Aside from school, which hangs like a pall
over most small boys, both red and white, and the shadow·of the truant
officer who was always in the offing, the boys lived ideal lives.

Riding down Seven Mile Wash one day I saw two Apache boys dart
into the brush ahead of me. I surmised that the two had run away from
school. When the boys saw who it was they came out in the open. "Excused," said one. "Sure you didn't run away from school?" Knowing
I wouldn't take him back, the youngster spoke again in apology: "Excused—damn lie," he said.

The outfit was eating dinner at headquarters when the truant officer
rode in with two boys who had run away from school and gone back to
the family wickiup about nine miles above the ranch. It was twelve more
miles down the wash to the Indian school at Rice and the day was hot
even for Arizona.

The truant officer was mounted; his two runaway boys, of about ten
and twelve years, walked ahead of him. The officer herded them into the
water corral, watered his charges out at the horse trough and was starting
down the wash again when we called them to come to our camp and eat.
The boys were barefoot, without hats, yet neither boy was sweating. The
runaways and the officer were joking with each other and aside from the
fact the officer rode a horse they might have been on some lark together.

The truant officer put away a bait that was in no way puny. But as
one of the punchers said—"them little ones et the big Indian right into
the ground." When a tobacco sack was passed the three rolled cigarettes
and they accepted chewing tobacco. "Damn near et the whole plug, too,"
said a puncher who had made the offering.

The Apaches, both men and women, are inveterate gamblers. While
I have never seen them line up and spit at a crack for money, like their
white brothers, the cowpunchers, they will gamble on anything. And to
"bet his shirt" is not just an expression with an Apache—at cards, a horse
race, a foot race. Most anything that was a gamble the Apache, no matter
how much or how little he had, always laid it on the line. It seemed to
make little difference if he won or lost. Nor did I ever hear a loser belly-
ache, it was the gamble he enjoyed.

When the El Capitan highway was built, only a small part went
through the reservation but many Apaches worked on the road. They

were good workers, too. Since the road went through a part of the old Bar F Bar range, the outfit occasionally camped on the water with the Apache workers and their families. One pay-day night the Apaches and punchers got together. A puncher had brought out a pair of boxing gloves from town and a fight was promoted. By the time the punchers and the Apaches got their money up, a little over a hundred dollars was involved.

When the Apaches picked the biggest Indian in the camp to represent them, a puncher, who was trying to get more money up, remarked to me: "That gut eater is big but he is packin' too much taller in the middle." The bronc peeler was to fight for the outfit. While outweighed by all of sixty pounds, like all his kind, he was made of whalebone and rawhide. And while the boxing gloves were as strange to him as to the Apache, the peeler was not without a local reputation. In town he seldom checked into a rooming house or hotel, it was money wasted since he usually spent the night in a local hoosegow for fighting on the street.

The foreman was picked to referee. His instructions were simple and to the point: there was to be no eye-gouging or biting nor could a man be kicked when he was down. A big fire was going. Cowpunchers, Apache men, women and children were gathered in a great circle. At first the Apaches stood silently, but as the punchers began yelling advice to their man, the Apaches, thinking it a part of the game, took it up, too. Indian dogs added to the commotion. One big mongrel mutt made a pass at the referee's leg and the belligerent pooch was promptly kicked out of the circle by a big Apache and the mutt went away howling. Finally the gloves were tied on and the referee once more repeated his instructions.

The big Apache came out pawing like a bear. The bronc peeler set himself, feinted, then whipped a left into the Apache's middle that seemed to disappear; a right to the jaw and it was over. The big Apache went down. There was no count, it wasn't necessary.

If there had been a racket before, bedlam broke loose now. An outsider would have found it hard to tell whose man had won. But the affair was not as one-sided as it might have been, for in the excitement that followed another big Indian dog that was on the prowl bit the winner in the leg.

Next the Apaches picked their fastest runner; a foot race was matched. The road was no boulevard, only partly graded and rough; it was up to the runners to pick their way through boulders and loose rock. But the moon was almost full. The foreman, who was to act as starter, stepped off a hundred yards. The Apache boy looked fast and since a cowpuncher afoot was seldom anything to brag about, the betting on the race was rather light as far as the outfit was concerned.

A cowboy named Young, better known as Brigham, volunteered to run for us. The Apache was running in his bare feet. As Brigham stumped off in his high-heeled boots with the foreman and the Apache to the starting line, he didn't look too good. I was ready to kiss the ten good-bye that I had won on the fight when a waddie beside me spoke. Evidently he was of the same mind but at least he offered consolation. "The Indian may beat him," said the puncher, "but Brigham has got ten dollars on hisself so we know it won't be pulled." Brigham took his boots off at the starting line and when the foreman fired the starting gun, that cowboy fairly flew.

The race was not even close, the Apache was simply outclassed. It was then that the Apaches did the thing I have never figured out. Every Apache insisted that he run Brigham for ten dollars. It was Brigham who finally called it off, after winning half a dozen races. His feet were pretty sore. But the Apaches would have kept it up all night and enjoyed each race as long as they had a dollar.

Next morning Brigham couldn't walk or ride, his boots had grown too small. That waddie luxuriated in his bed and many times that day he counted the dough he'd won. That night in camp around the fire there were no pitching horses rode or big steers roped and tied. The doings of the night before were all hashed over again; the fight, each race that Brigham won was run again. But why would even an Apache make a bet when he knew he couldn't win? We gave it up. We were turning in when one of the old punchers spoke. "Anyway," he said, "it clears up a lot of things for me; now I can understand why the Apache was always rooked an' why he always got the worst of it in his dealings with the white man."

APACHE LAND

II

AN APACHE must never look at his mother-in-law nor is he allowed to speak to her, either; it is simply an expression of respect. When the mother-in-law enters a wickiup or dwelling, the son-in-law must leave at once. In traveling together in a wagon or car, a curtain is hung between them. One can't help but speculate as to when and why the custom originated. And since it was customary in former times for an Apache to have two or three wives, one can imagine the husband a busy man in camp simply avoiding his various mothers-in-law.

The son was lost to his family by marriage as henceforth his obligations were to the family of his wife. Should the wife die, the husband was supposed to remain in mourning for a year; then he usually married a sister of his former wife or one of her cousins.

In marriage the consent of the girl's parents was necessary. One of the suitor's relatives did the honors. After her family had been notified, the real proposal came in the form of presents, usually in horses. Since the suitor was supposed to offer as many horses as he could afford, it was seldom a "one-horse affair."

At night the ponies were tied outside or near the girl's wickiup. If the girl fed the horses and took them to water, the suitor was accepted. The horses were seldom cared for on the first day but if left uncared for on the second day, she was considered snooty. If, however, the horses were not fed or taken to water at the end of the fourth day, his suit was rejected. There was nothing for him to do but come and get his ponies. How the rejected suitor may have felt is only surmise but it's a cinch he was in better shape than the neglected horses.

If the suitor was accepted, it was followed by three days of feasting. On the third night the couple slipped away to a temporary wickiup that was, supposedly, hidden. After a week or two they returned and built their wickiup near that of the mother-in-law. Nowadays they live in either

family group and marriages are performed according to white standards. When I asked an old Apache friend if the custom had always been adhered to, he laughed. "Apache boy and girl all the same white boy and girl. Lots of times know they get married before parents know."

The family unit consisted of grandparents, unmarried sons and daughters' married daughters and their husbands, and the daughters' children. They lived in large family groups. The home of the mother was the family center; cousins were called brother or sister. Blood ties run deep in Apaches.

After the family came the local group of families who might or might not be related. If it was to their mutual interests, anyone might join the group. Each family had a head man or spokesman and there was always one who spoke for the affiliated family groups or the clan. A man became a spokesman or leader simply on merit. There were no hereditary chiefs unless the sons, themselves, proved leadership. There was real democracy among the Apaches and if a leader failed he was quickly dropped and ignored.

The clan was always designated by a name descriptive of their location. It might be a canyon, mountain, river or spring. The family groups or clan were always cooperative; women found it to their advantage to work together at gathering nuts, acorns and wild food as well as gathering mescal and roasting it in the great pits. These pits were quite common on the range. Many are found on Mescal Mountain. With their black, burned rocks they are often mistaken by the uninitiated for small, extinct volcanic craters.

A band was composed of several family groups or clans and from these bands came the tribal organization. While each clan or band was highly mobile and their economy was always geared for war, as a people the Apaches were loosely united. The Apache's first allegiance was to his family and his clan. It was seldom the clans or bands were all united. Even in an emergency they never went "all out." While they spoke the same language and, for the most part, their customs were the same, many bands had no contact with each other except through individuals. And if a clan or band encroached on another's preserve they would fight each other as quickly as they would the Mexicans or Americans.

The Apache believes in a supreme being called Usen who is the giver of all life and who is of no sex or place, nor can the Apache approach this power directly. The power must work through something and every Apache is a potential recipient. The agent of this power is revealed through dreams and visions and the agent may come in many forms: through certain animals, the snake, the sun, the lightning, or even an insect. Whatever agent through which this power is revealed becomes the Apache's guardian spirit or his medicine.

A deeply religious person, the Apache has ceremonies that cover almost everything from curing disease to finding lost objects. The ceremonies may consist of singing and dancing or smoking. Pollen is used in most ceremonies. There were certain ceremonies that called for the services of a medicine man who wielded a powerful influence among his people. Nor does the medicine man function for nothing; he is always paid for his services. As a usual thing a ceremony for curing sickness is held for one person. But there are rites given during an epidemic for the whole community and there are ceremonies for protection from snakes, scorpions and the lightning.

Several years ago a friend witnessed a ceremony near the old Cross S horse camp on the mountain. The medicine man was to bring rain. It was that time of year, too, when the thunderheads begin boiling up over the mountain. The medicine man addressed his people, stating in no

uncertain terms that if there was any levity or anything done to displease him he would call it off. As he talked, my friend observed, the medicine man kept an eye cocked on the thunderheads and they were boiling. The medicine man knew his clouds, so did my friend who had spent years on the mountain. He was just as quick to spot the break in the clouds as the medicine man who said, immediately, that some of his people had displeased him and he called the whole thing off.

Sometime about 1915 or '16, word spread among the San Carlos Apaches that there was to be a great flood. Most of the Indians moved their wickiups to higher ground. It finally reached the local papers. That summer in camp, cowpunchers argued pro and con, made bets on whether the Apaches were right or wrong. Some old-timers said the Apaches knew about such things. Others argued just as stoutly that they didn't. It was a wet summer; Gilson, Seven Mile and all the washes ran many times, and while there was never the big washout, it furnished a new topic of conversation in the outfit. At the first drop of rain some waddie would remark, "Here she comes an' it's me for the high country."

Since rain or lack of it can mean life or death, it was only natural during a drouthy period or dry year that the Apache medicine man was often a topic of conversation in the outfit. Most punchers were doubting Thomases who scoffed, yet there were always some who believed and would cite specific instances as proof. One drouthy year, with cattle dying, I heard an old cowman say in all seriousness: "Reckon the white

God has throwed us down, I'm stringin' along with the medicine man."

Pollen seems to have great importance as a ceremonial offering. Corn is often used and the medicine feather, a soft, downy feather that comes from the eagle. There are ceremonial hoops, some only a few inches in diameter, some a foot or more, painted in various colors. And there are painted staffs, three or four feet long. Placed on a sick person, the illness is supposed to leave with the removal of the objects. Many ceremonies have their own equipment: shells, turquoise, often parts of animals such as the head of a quail, the claw of an animal.

Lee Hickman, an old friend, witnessed a ceremony where live rattlesnakes were used. During the ceremony an Apache child of about three or four years was bitten and the medicine man immediately took the child into a tepee; no one else went inside. The next morning Lee saw the child playing about, apparently none the worse for the experience. Lee speculated, too, as to whether the poison had been taken from the rattlesnakes before the ceremony. But Lee also said that after what he saw, in case of snake bite, he'd string along with a medicine man if he could get him.

Most Apache ceremonies have been interpreted and recorded by learned men; however, they were always confusing to me. The more I watched an Apache ceremony the less I knew for sure. It may have been my approach. As a small boy I attended church with my mother and, while it was always under protest, the attendance was regular. Since I sat and squirmed through the entire proceedings I fear the message fell on fallow ground. But by simply watching the minister's movements about the rostrum I came to know just what period his discourse had reached. Even without the sound of his voice, by simply watching the movement of his feet and counting so many paces, I knew when he was tapering off. And when he moved five paces to the left and once more stood directly behind his pulpit, I knew it wouldn't be much longer. Nor will I ever forget the new minister who came. His movements about the rostrum meant absolutely nothing so far as timing his discourse went; as a matter of fact, he always crossed me up. Somehow I always felt the same way in watching an Apache ceremony.

When an Apache girl reaches functional maturity, a coming-out party is held. We often attended these parties and there is one, long remembered, a friend and I attended on Cibecue given by old R 14 for two of his nieces. Since Old R 14 was the wealthiest Apache on either reservation, owning thousands of cattle, the old boy put it on big.

Many old-time white cowmen started with only a good pony, a long rope and a running iron and eventually became wealthy. But Old R 14 started with one black Mexican cow. The black cow was issued for beef by the government and R 14 did a strange and unheard-of thing for an Apache at that time. Instead of killing and eating the critter, he kept her. The black cow had a calf. It was the start, the beginning of his herd. Other beef issued by the government he kept, too, and it was only a few years until he was selling beef back to the government. How he supplemented his own meat larder during this period is only surmise. It is a question to this day that is better left unasked of any cowman.

Old R 14 had become a legend even when I met him over twenty years ago. It was said that our beneficent government, on learning that an Apache had a good-sized herd of cattle, sent R 14 several fine young Hereford bulls. R 14 promptly had them all castrated, saying that anything would do for a bull but these young Herefords would make good steers, which were the animals sold for beef. Be that as it may, he prospered. Eventually he hired a white man to run his outfit who not only ran it well but as the business grew with all its complications he became Old R 14's friend and adviser as well.

For days every horse and rider, every wagon on the upper reservation had been heading for the rendezvous at Cibecue. When my friend and I arrived, hundreds of Apaches were camped about the place. Old R 14 sat in front of his wickiup like a great black Buddha and welcomed all who came. Meat was hanging over wagon bows, on bushes, it was hanging everywhere; even the dogs were full, for R 14 had killed many beeves for the party.

There were not over a half dozen whites present, mostly cowpunchers. And all day long, for three days, Apaches and white punchers roped calves, team-tied, and filled their bellies with beef. The setting was a natural amphitheatre, a great bowl with the red of the soil always in contrast to the green of the cedars and the great dome of the blue sky overhead. Our little campfire was only one of many. As night fell quickly, as it always does in this country, the little fires danced like so many fireflies on the edge of the great bowl.

A big pile of wood had been gathered, as darkness fell it was lighted. The slow rhythm of the drums began and from each little fire came Apaches, singly and in groups, to gather in a great circle. Then came an Apache voice in song rising above the sound of the drums. As the voice rose and fell it was not unlike that of the singer's brother, the coyote. It was the social dance and R 14's nieces appeared as if from nowhere, carrying staffs and the small hoops; each girl had a medicine feather in her sleek black hair. Their dresses were ankle-length and elaborately decorated, they wore turquoise as well as gadgets from the five and ten cent store. With their eager faces and their strong young bodies they were something to admire.

Now an old Apache, his coarse black hair streaked with gray, harangued the audience; he spoke at some length, too. When at the end

of his talk I asked an Apache what was said, he informed me, curtly, that the speaker was talking to his people. I had already surmised as much, knowing if it was meant for the white cowpunchers he would have spoken in English. Having no friends among the White Mountain Apaches, I retired, thinking I might have spoken out of turn. But the Apache I had questioned followed me and spoke almost apologetically: the speaker had said that the married women could dance, too, if they left the kids out of it and he had also said that the Apaches were to dance with the cowboys, to see that the white cowpunchers had a good time.

The Apache men sat around the fire and, as my friend said, looked for all the world as if they were waiting for a rat to come out of a hole. As they were tapped to dance by the women many did not even look up, yet they immediately went directly to the women who had tapped them and danced the four-four beat, back and forth. Nor did the Apache cut a rug or squall as is often the custom of his white brother, the cowpuncher, when he stomps the floor at a baile. Occasionally, two girls would tap one man and as the three danced back and forth, with arms folded, to the four-four beat, the girls sometimes giggled and laughed; but on the whole it looked to be a serious affair. It was amusing when two Apache girls tapped a six-foot-three cowpuncher; the girls were fussed and giggling, but as for the puncher, he came through.

About midnight there was a visible stir as the devil dancers appeared out of the darkness. Four masked figures, carrying wooden swords, they wore towering, painted wooden headdress, short buckskin skirts and moccasins; their bodies naked and painted from the waist up. With them was the clown; his entire body painted, he wore little except the clout, but he, too, carried a wooden sword. As they moved clockwise around the circle they seemed to be forever hunting something that could not be found and their "Hoo-hoo" sounded much like the low hooting of an owl.

There were countless songs and verses. The night was cool; many Apaches wore blankets but the bodies of the devil dancers glistened with sweat. And through it all, the social dance and the devil dance, the two debutantes danced together in slow cadence. In the great circle women nursed babies on cradle-boards, exhausted children slept. During the excitement of the first appearance of the devil dancers there was a dog fight, but the belligerent pooches were unceremoniously kicked out of the circle.

About three A.M. my friend and I spread our blankets. The sky was showing gray in the east and the drums were still going when I sat up to roll a cigarette. All about us were sleeping Apaches. Not ten feet from our camp, an Apache boy, still in his teens, was rolled in a blanket. As I smoked, he came alive. He simply unrolled himself; he had slept with his hat on and was fully dressed. He had his bridle in his hand and as I watched he went off to catch his horse. Soon the dead fires about us began to smoke. There was the smell of coffee and of frying meat as the new day began.

Aside from the color and the pageantry that is unforgettable, the one thing that always impressed me most at their dances was the order of it all. Let that many white cowpunchers rope and ride for three days and dance for three nights and there would be arguments, fights aplenty. During the three days and nights I heard not a single argument, the only fights were put on by the dogs. I saw only two old bucks sleeping off the effects of what was, apparently, not soda pop or "bellywash."

My friend and I were not on hand for the final ceremony when the debutantes received their last instructions—dancing at the west end of the circle in front of the medicine man, facing the rising sun. Nor did we see the pollen sprinkled at the symbolic wickiup that had been erected,

where the pile of blankets was torn apart, one thrown in each direction or
to the four winds. After all, three days of roping and riding and three
nights of dancing will wear a person down. My friend and I slept through
it all.

The medicine feather, that soft, downy feather that comes from the
eagle, is highly prized by the Apaches. They are worn during most ceremonies. I have seen them tied to cradle-boards to keep the baby healthy
and strong, and I have seen them tied to a pony's mane before a race.

One winter I trapped with a friend on Sycamore. We were trapping

for coyotes and, by accident, we caught two eagles at the carcass of a
wild burro. We gave the medicine feathers to the Apaches and one,
James K. Polk, was so grateful he promised to sing four songs for my
friend. "Me sing four songs," said James K. Polk, "me sing four songs."

We promptly forgot all about the medicine feathers. They may be
good luck to an Apache but seemed to work in reverse as far as a white
man is concerned, at least they did in our case. We were trying to crank
the flivver one cold November morning, without jacking up the hind
wheel, when an Apache who was camped with his family on the water
above us appeared. "Tomorrow Habbensgibben," he said, "lice all gone
on me, feel pretty good." Since we didn't even know the day of the week
we had no idea that the next day was Thanksgiving, but we decided if it
meant enough for an Apache to delouse himself, we should do something
about it, too.

We finally decided to go into town and buy a chicken as relief from
our straight diet of beef. We knew we would be thrown bodily out of any
restaurant in town and we intended to bring the chicken back to camp
to cook. A trapper always smells to high heaven and there's a reason.

Aside from the coyote smell that is forever with him, most trappers have a "scent" the secret of which is guarded with their lives. The base for it is usually dog or coyote urine since the coyote has many of the same habits of his half brother, the dog. And it is knowing these habits that makes the successful trapper.

It always amused me at the ranch to watch a trapper who had tied his dog up for the night, follow his pooch with a plate when the dog was turned loose for his morning's morning. My friend and partner was resourceful. He tied old Brownie, the trap dog, up in the tent for the night, but he had acquired a piece of inner tube he tied on Brownie where it would do the most good before he turned him out in the morning. After the hound had kicked the bushes to his heart's content, my friend simply poured the contents of the inner tube into a bottle.

When we got to town I did not leave the car while my friend went to the butcher shop. But all the town dogs who didn't follow him came boiling up the street, their hair all turned the wrong way, surrounded the car and barked at me. Later, a friend told me all the dogs in town were still barking two hours after we left.

We saw the engine a mile above the Trading Post but we had no idea that the crossing was blocked. As we turned the lights dimmed, whatever my friend stepped on was evidently the wrong thing. I thought at first we had gone completely through the coke car that blocked the siding, but we only made it half way. We backed the flivver out with the help of the train crew and finally herded it into the corral by the Post. My friend was a good mechanic, the trader carried parts, and we worked all next day. That evening we were ready to go back to camp when we saw James K. Polk riding towards us down the wash. He wore the medicine feathers about his neck; he waved and smiled from ear to ear as he passed. "That's the damn Indian who promised to sing for me," said my friend; and, as an afterthought, he added: "He sing four songs and it cost me forty dollars."

SOME HISTORY

III

THE Apache and Navajo are said to be cousins, yet there is little resemblance today. Just where and when the two tribes split is not known. Nor do the learned men agree as to when the Apache first came to the Southwest. Some say the Apache was here at the coming of the Spaniards, others say at that date the Apache was still working his way down from the Far North. But by the middle of the seventeenth century he had occupied all of New Mexico, a large portion of west Texas, all of southern Arizona and the States of Sonora and Chihuahua in Old Mexico.

Never a pastoral people, always on the move, his economy geared for war, the Apache roamed this vast territory, raiding and fighting the Pueblos and all the desert tribes until Mexico became the real Apache commissary.

The Apaches called themselves Tinneh, Inde or Dinneh, meaning "the people." The word Apache is of Spanish origin, believed to be a corruption of the Zuni word "enemy." Castañeda, chronicler for Coronado, first mentions the name in 1580. And of all the Indians who occupied the Southwest, the Apache proved himself the wildest, fiercest, cruelest, above all the wiliest. While he constantly raided the Pueblos, he aligned himself with these people during the great Pueblo revolt in 1680, and again in 1745 and 1750 when they attempted to throw off the yoke of the Spaniards.

The entreaties of the Jesuits and Franciscans fell on deaf ears as far as the Apache was concerned. Always deep in the Apache consciousness was the unforgettable memory of what happened to any Indian who made contact with these white intruders. The Apache had, no doubt, seen the Spanish brand on cheek or hip of Indians herded onto the plantations or into the mines to work and die as slaves. Roaming the hills and the high country with the bear, the wolf, the mountain lion and his

brother, the coyote, the Apache would not be conquered or confined by
the Spanish nor later by the Mexicans.

Always a fighter, the Apache from earliest boyhood was trained in

an age-old school of savagery. Of pity he had none, to a captive the
Apache was merciless. If an Apache wanted information from an enemy,
the tortures were unspeakable. To spread-eagle a captive over an ant hill,
smearing the captive's eyes and mouth with honey, was said to be one
favorite. Another was to hang a prisoner head down over a slow fire while

the squaws skinned him alive. If a captive was too young to travel, the child's brains were bashed out against a rock. When boys and girls were taken who were old enough to withstand the hardships of the trail they were adopted into the tribe and treated by the Apaches as they did their own children. Many captives rose to a position of influence in the tribe and many Mexicans captured as children became Apache warriors.

The Apache knew every trail of the great territory he roamed, and he traveled light. With his bow and quiver of arrows, later a gun and ammunition, a knife, a little pinole or jerky; dressed only in a clout and with moccasins that reached to his thigh, he carried his sacred amulets—a splinter of a tree struck by lightning, the head of a bird, the claw of an animal or whatever his medicine might be. With his deep chest and tireless legs he was capable of traveling great distances afoot, often as much as seventy-five miles a day in an emergency.

The Apache seldom attacked in the open. He was a master strategist. It was said that one Apache lurking in the vicinity was enough to demoralize the affairs of an entire Pueblo and, later, an entire Mexican village.

To get himself killed with a show of bravado was the last thing the Apache had on his mind. He was never foolhardy and only when wounded to the death would an Apache fight to the finish. Nighttime was sacred to his ancestral dead, the Apache seldom struck until dawn. Unlike the Plains Indians, the Apache seldom took a scalp and as the settlements grew he found it was "bad medicine" to burn a ranchhouse or building as it soon set enemies in motion on his trail.

When followed in force the Apaches scattered like a covey of quail only to meet again at a designated spot. In both following a trail and eluding his pursuers the Apache was a past master. Knowing the habits of every animal and with his knowledge of wild foods, the Apache roamed his great range at will, since his wants were always simple. During the season he might plant a patch of corn, melons, squash and beans in some remote fastness. He made flour of the acorns but mescal was his real staple. Game was plentiful, the bow and arrow killed silently. But with the introduction of livestock to his world in mules, horses, cattle, sheep and goats, Mexico became his real commissary since meat was his favorite food and raiding his very life.

Mule meat was said to be his preference, then the horse and the cow. An American traveler in the early '50's who visited the Apaches on the

Gila tells of hearing the screams of a mule. Upon investigation he found the Apaches had tied the animal down and were cutting steaks from the live mule's flanks; when the traveler asked why, he was told the meat was more tender that way.

Unlike the Plains Indians, the Apache was not a good horseman. His fondness for horsemeat, evidently, offset any aversion he might have for traveling afoot.

The Spaniards' only use for any Indians was as slaves for the plantations or in the mines. The Mexicans, finding they could not exterminate or conquer the Apaches, tried at times to get along. For quite a period the State of Chihuahua made peace and issued rations while, at the same time, the Apaches were at war with the neighboring State of Sonora. Stock stolen by the Apaches in Sonora was sold to Mexicans in Chihuahua. This method of appeasement caused only more contempt in the Apache heart for the race that he despised.

Apaches were so bold as to appear in small groups outside Mexican settlements, killing the herders and running off livestock in broad daylight. When pursued by troops in force the Apaches scattered, leaving no trail; if the pursuing force was small and diligent, it was often led into ambush and wiped out by the Indians. It was about this time that the Mexican States offered a bounty for Apache scalps, one hundred pesos for a man's, fifty pesos for a woman's. How the authorities distinguished between the scalp of a man or woman has never been explained. But for a short time the scalp industry flourished, even bringing in some American scalp hunters.

One James Kirker organized a company. Kirker's outfit brought in so many scalps the Mexican government refused to pay the full amount. It was said that Kirker and Co. were none too fastidious, bringing in Mexican scalps as well. And there were the partners, Johnson and Gleason, who went into the business of scalp hunting in a big way.

Johnson was a friend of Juan Jose, one of the noted Apache chiefs of his day. Making a deal with the Mexican government, Johnson betrayed his Apache friend, inviting the chief and his people to a feast at the old Santa Rita Mine in New Mexico. While Apache men, women and children were happily eating, Johnson touched off a small, hidden field piece in their midst that was loaded with slugs and scrap iron, killing Apache men, women and children by the score and wounding scores

of others, who were promptly dispatched on the spot.

In the meantime Johnson's partner, Gleason, had taken Juan Jose aside to dicker for a saddle mule, and when Johnson touched off the field piece, Gleason shot the chief. Badly wounded, Juan Jose grappled with Gleason, at the same time calling for his friend, Johnson, to come to his aid. Johnson came on the run, shooting his friend, the chief, through the head with a pistol.

History does not tell what happened to Johnson and Gleason but it does record the passing of Glanton, another Apache scalp and bounty hunter of note. Glanton and his party had made their way across Arizona to the Colorado River. Word of Glanton's head-hunting business, however, had preceded him. Yuma Indians allowed the party to start across the river by boat, then from ambush the Indians wiped Glanton and his party out. As a solution, the bounty on Apache scalps by the Mexican States was a failure since the Apaches intensified their raids.

It was during this period the Apache learned much about the character of the new invader from the North, the American. Some Apaches, however, were slow to learn.

Mangas Coloradas, who succeeded Juan Jose, was said to be a giant in stature and intellect as well, yet he walked unarmed with a flag of truce into a camp of American prospectors where he was promptly seized, bound, hung by the wrists and whipped until he was insensible. On regaining consciousness he was allowed to drag his battered body from the camp to the accompaniment of jeers from the Americans. Nor did Mangas Coloradas ever learn; in his dealings with Americans the chief was always naive. Like Juan Jose, he was murdered, too; not by renegade Americans and Mexicans, however, but by soldiers of the California Volunteers when he was enticed into their camp on a pretense of friendship.

All in all, it sounds like a dirty business on both sides and it was. The more one digs into the record, the worse it becomes. The Apache was a savage, yet for any act of savagery on the part of the Apache we were able to match it tenfold. Colonel John R. Baylor, Confederate soldier and gentleman and Governor of Arizona Territory during the War Between the States, was relieved of the governorship and his commission by Jefferson Davis for having flour poisoned and killed some fifty-odd Indians. The Navajos, cousins of the Apaches, fared equally as well when whites placed strychnine in watermelons and killed them as they would poison coyotes.

And there was the "Pinole Treaty" by King Woolsey. Invited to eat pinole and hold a powwow with the whites, wounded Apaches who were not killed by the first fire dragged themselves up the wash and died in the rock tanks where the water ran red with blood. To this day the wash is known as Bloody Tanks. Woolsey was given an ovation by the Territorial Legislature after this affair.

And there was the party, later to be known as the Camp Grant Massacre, when Papagoes, Mexicans and Americans, led by two of Tucson's leading citizens, attacked a sleeping camp of peaceful Aravaipa Apaches, killing eight men and over one hundred women and children.

While always at war with the Mexicans, the chroniclers tell us the mountain men, the trappers, the first Americans from the North, were well received by the Apaches. These men wanted no land nor did they search for the white metal (gold). Apaches welcomed General Kearny and his soldiers as an ally against the Mexicans. Even with the coming of the prospectors and the colonists the Apache was slow to learn that there was little difference between his hereditary enemy, the Mexican, and the invaders from the North.

We inherited the Apache and all his great domain at the close of the Mexican War by the Treaty of Guadalupe Hidalgo, in 1848. By the terms we naively accepted responsibility for the Apaches in both the

United States and Mexico. Nor was the Apache, who controlled most of this great land, consulted in any way. On the whole we accepted a large order that was not entirely settled even when Geronimo was deported from Arizona and shipped East in 1886. Since our dual policy of civilian and military control was confounding to most Americans, it is small wonder the Apache was bewildered by it all. When the San Carlos Reservation was established in 1872 there were five successive agents, three civilian and two military, during a period of eighteen months.

It was during the period of the War Between the States that the Apaches reached their greatest peak in war. Cochise, chief of the fighting Chiricahuas, had always been friendly to the Americans. Mangas Coloradas, chief of the Warm Springs band, in spite of his bloody beating by the prospectors, had tried to get along. A tactless blunder by a young lieutenant, only two years out of West Point, started the long and bloody war.

The young lieutenant and a company of soldiers were in search of a Mexican boy and livestock that had been stolen by raiding Apaches. Inviting Cochise and several members of his family inside the tent, and after soldiers had surrounded it, the lieutenant accused Cochise of the theft. Cochise denied any knowledge of the affair. Later it was proven that Cochise spoke the truth. Accused by the young lieutenant of lying and told that he and his party would be held as hostages until the boy and livestock were returned, Cochise escaped at once. Capturing three white men, he attempted to make an exchange of prisoners. When the young lieutenant refused, Cochise put his captors to a cruel death, after which the soldiers hung three of Cochise's relatives, two nephews and his brother.

When Cochise took to the warpath he vowed that for every Apache killed in the fighting ten whites would pay with their lives. It is said he more than made good his word. Joined by Mangas Coloradas and his band, they raided far and wide. When Federal troops were withdrawn from Arizona at the beginning of the War Between the States, the Apaches, thinking they had driven the invaders out, redoubled their efforts. Arizona was devastated.

With the coming of the California Column to Arizona in 1862, the fighting reached its highest peak. When Apaches attacked the Column in Apache Pass, it was only with the aid of two howitzers brought up by the Column that the Americans were finally victorious.

Mangas Coloradas was severely wounded in this fight, the Apaches badly mauled. Not long after this fight Mangas Coloradas and his Warm Springs band withdrew, but Cochise and his fighting Chiricahuas carried on alone. Cochise and his Chiricahuas were still fighting when President Grant sent General O. O. Howard to Arizona in 1872 to make peace with Cochise and his band and to give them a reservation. The tragic blunder one young lieutenant made that day in 1861 had paid frightful dividends.

It was in the early '70's that the policy of placing Apaches on reservations really began to take shape. Until this time they had no way to turn, caught between the Mexican on the south and the American on the north; the Apaches as a people were being slowly ground to bits.

When the account of the Camp Grant Massacre appeared in the papers it caused such a storm of protest in the East that with President Grant's approval a permanent board of Peace Commissioners was formed. The object of the commission was justice for the Indians. Yet when Vincent Colyer, the Quaker, who was a member of President Grant's Commission, came to Arizona to lay out the reservations, the *Arizona Miner,* in Prescott, in an editorial offered two suggestions: one, that Colyer either be stoned to death or dumped down a mine shaft. While the *Tucson Citizen* was vituperative, it was not so violent. Citizens in the Territory wanted no reservations. Their solution was nothing short of the extermination of the Apaches.

It was in the early '70's, too, that General Crook was assigned to Arizona. Called Nantan Lupin (the Gray Wolf) by the Apaches, Crook's policy was one they understood: either come into the reservations and live in peace or be exterminated. Crook, more than any other soldier, was respected by the Apaches; Crook spoke simply to them and he always spoke the truth. Tireless as the Apache scouts he enlisted, Crook was always in the field. On the reservations he counseled them in peace. To Crook the Apache was a human being; from personal contacts he knew the ones who wanted peace and he knew the renegades. He wanted the Apache to be self-supporting, raise livestock, feed and grain. It was this policy that drew the fire from citizens in the Territory. Army contracts at this time were the source of the citizens' largest revenues.

Crook had settled fifteen hundred Rio Verdes at Camp Verde on a reservation of their own. Crook told the Rio Verdes that with whites crowding into the Territory they could not live on game; he advised them to raise horses, cows and sheep, plant crops and farm. At Crook's suggestion the Rio Verdes dug an irrigation ditch over five miles in length. The ditch averaged four feet in width and was three feet in depth. With old, worn-out army equipment, spades and axes, even sticks hardened in the fire, bucks sweated in the sun; in baskets the squaws packed out the dirt. Fields were put in and planted. Yet before the crops could be harvested our government not only changed its mind, it broke its sacred word. Crook protested bitterly but the Rio Verdes were rounded up and herded to San Carlos.

White Mountain Apaches and Chiricahuas were rounded up, taken from their reservations, and sent to San Carlos, too. In each instance our government broke its solemn word. In our stupid and pinch-penny policy with the Apaches, the transfer of Victorio and his Warm Springs band from New Mexico proved quite expensive. Victorio was Mangas Coloradas' successor and Victorio did not stay at San Carlos long. Rallying his fighting men, he made his greatest raids. New Mexico and Chihuahua, Mexico, were once more drenched in blood. Nor did Victorio ask for peace; he fought until he died.

Almost a year after Victorio was killed in Old Mexico, Old Nana, his lieutenant, made one final, desperate raid. Old Nana was in his seventies and so racked with rheumatism it was an effort to mount a horse. Coming out of Old Mexico with only fifteen men, he raided twelve hundred miles. Old Nana and his little band averaged seventy-five miles a day; leaving a trail of bloodshed and outwitting the troops who followed him, he returned to Mexico in safety.

The basic trouble lay in Washington; no place in our dealings with the Apache was a clear-cut policy carried through for any length of time. The Department of the Interior and the Department of War were constantly at loggerheads and both departments responded to pressure groups in contemporary fashion.

The reservation at San Carlos was an empire in itself, roughly over a hundred miles square. In the northern end of the reservation were many mountain streams that were fed from the snows of mountains that towered eleven thousand feet. Piñon, pine and juniper abounded on the slopes. Black River, a mountain stream, divided the reservation. On the Gila that formed the boundary on the south, snow seldom came and the sun was always warm.

When the San Carlos Reservation was given to the Apaches in 1872, it was a no-man's land. With the discovery of minerals at the western boundary, the whites came pouring in. One of the earliest arrivals from Silver City, New Mexico, an enterprising man, brought whiskey in quantities along with many sacks of potatoes. Having no liquor license he sold his potatoes at a dollar and a half apiece and with each sale he donated a pint of whiskey as a goodwill offering. But the resident from Silver City did not have long to wait until he could legalize his trade. What became the Globe district, with its silver deposits and later the great bodies of copper ore, was promptly taken from the Apaches and given to the whites.

When silver was found at what is now the ghost town of McMillen, it, too, was chiseled off; as were the great ore deposits in the Clifton-Morenci district. In all, five cuts were made. Land-hungry Mormons from Utah came south and took up land. Cowmen moved in with their herds. Even to this day there are cowmen who look with longing eye at the great Apache range. That the "gut-eaters" should be raising cattle of their own—and good ones, too, well, it doesn't make sense to them.

Had General Crook, with his understanding of the Apache problem, stayed in Arizona things might have gone along. With Crook's departure to take over the Department of the Platte, in 1875, things went from bad to worse.

While many renegades still roamed the hills, when Crook left for the North, the Apaches as a whole were on the reservation. Agents came and agents went. Many were honorable men; some, however, were so dishonest as to leave a stench in the nostrils of citizens of the Territory who hated and despised the Apache. One agent, Tiffany by name, was such a rascal as to be indicted by a Federal grand jury. While he was agent he went into the cow business, his herd being acquired from cattle bought for the Apaches. Supplies for the Apaches were freighted to Globe and sold at night. There was a mine the agent worked on the reservation, some of his partners reached all the way to Washington. Nor could an Apache protest. Apaches were held in jail for months at a time on any excuse, nor was there any hearing. Bewildered by it all, the Apaches had no place to turn. The wonder is that more of them did not break out and go back to their life of raiding.

The Apaches were issued rations, whether they received the full allotment depended on the agent's whim; according to the setup, even a nursing babe was entitled to a sack of flour and its quota of fresh beef. Nor was the Apache encouraged to raise livestock or be diligent in any way. In many instances fields planted by Apaches were deliberately destroyed. For the Apaches to be self-supporting was the last thing that was wanted. It was a paradise for thieving men and crooks. While the Apaches were left holding the sack, contractors, agents and higher-ups in Washington were riding the gravy train.

The San Carlos stench finally reached the nostrils of the Honorable Carl Schurtz, then Secretary of the Interior, and to his everlasting credit he used the axe at once; heads fell all along the way, including the agent at San Carlos and the Commissioner of Indian Affairs in Washington.

Indian agents, however, were always underpaid, and as small politi-
cos, graft was always a temptation when the "gravy" was in sight. But
there were honest agents. One of the most outstanding during the long
period at San Carlos was young Agent John P. Clum, who clashed at
every turn with the military. Clum may have had his faults. A contro-
versial person in Arizona to this day, even his enemies admitted that
Clum was an honest man. It was Clum who organized the Apache Police,
set up their own courts and juries where the Apaches could, as far as
practical, administer their own affairs. And like General Crook, Clum
wanted the Apaches to be self-supporting; buying livestock for them, he
bought hay and grain from the Apaches, too. In this Clum brought down
the wrath of the citizens of the Territory who wanted contracts with the
government for feeding these people they hated and despised. Clum not
only clashed with the military, he clashed with the civil authorities in
Washington. Since there was only one thing on the young agent's mind,
the welfare of the Apaches, one wonders on reading the record how he
lasted three long years.

General Crook was reassigned to the command in Arizona in 1882.
During his absence since 1875 conditions had grown steadily worse.

Small wonder the Apaches were restless and bewildered by it all. It
was rumored their reservation was to be taken from them and the entire
tribe deported East. Until General Crook's return to Arizona it had not
occurred to anyone to learn the Apaches' side of the story. General Crook
knew more Apaches personally than any man or officer of his day. He
was constantly in the saddle, interviewing Apache leaders, listening to
their stories. But General Crook had come too late to make any peaceful
solution of the mess. Most Apaches were "fed up" and especially the
Chiricahuas.

Always the most warlike of the Apaches, they had been taken from
their reservation, deeded to them in solemn treaty by our government,
and herded to San Carlos. Several hundred Chiricahuas had been located
on the upper reservation near the White River sub-agency.

Chato, a young chief, and twenty-six warriors were the first to break
out. The chief of police had attempted to arrest a young buck for a trivial
offense. The Chiricahuas had no quarrel over the arrest but when the
young buck ran into a group of squaws and children and the chief of

police fired at the young buck and killed a woman instead, the Apaches became highly incensed. A few days later they waylaid the chief of police, killing him and cutting off his head. After kicking the head about and using it as a football, they high-tailed it for Mexico, leaving the usual trail of bloodshed through southern Arizona.

Organizing a force of one hundred and ninety-three Apache scouts and with one company of the Sixth Cavalry, Crook took the field himself, trailing the renegades two hundred miles below the international border to the headwaters of the Yaqui River. Here he surprised and whipped the renegades in a short, decisive fight, bringing them back to San Carlos where they were put to work at hard labor.

In 1882, Geronimo and Nachee, the son of Cochise, left the reservation with a considerable force of Chiricahuas and headed into Mexico, then surrendered to Crook and were returned in 1883. In May, 1885, Geronimo and Nachee broke out again, taking one hundred and twenty-four men, women and children. They left the usual trail of blood as they dashed for Old Mexico. Chato, however, and two-thirds of the Chiricahuas remained. Chato did not like Geronimo. Enlisted as a scout by Crook, Chato served faithfully and remained friendly to the whites.

On Geronimo's outbreak in '85, thirty-nine whites were murdered in New Mexico, thirty-four in Arizona. When the renegades slipped back and raided an Apache village near Camp Apache, the raiders killed twelve friendly Apaches and carried off six women and children.

From 1882 to 1886 is known in Apache history as the period of the Geronimo unrest. It is ironical that Geronimo should be the leading figure. Geronimo may have taken a leaf from the white man's book; among the Apache leaders there was one thing that set him apart. Geronimo was a liar who never spoke the truth. A medicine man who rose as a leader, his people feared him, too. But Geronimo was the rallying point for all the disillusioned and the malcontents.

Geronimo, a southern Chiricahua, surrendered many times to the military but he was captured only once and then by young civilian Agent John P. Clum and Clay Beauford, who was captain of the Apache Police. The capture was made at Ojo Caliente, New Mexico, in 1877. Geronimo, who was not well known at this time, was taken to San Carlos in irons.

Agent Clum's recommendation that the rascal be tried in civil court for crimes committed in the Territory might have solved the problem. But in no time Geronimo was out of the guardhouse and receiving his rations the same as any peaceful Apache. His games of hide and seek with General Crook are history. Geronimo usually stayed out until such time as he wanted rations again. Returning to the reservation with many promises of good behavior on his part, he stayed until he felt the urge to raid and kill again; then promptly broke his word.

The old renegade was cagy, too; when he surrendered in Mexico he always picked the ground of his own choosing. In '86, when General Crook went into Mexico to receive Geronimo's surrender, according to Geronimo's terms, General Crook and his party went unarmed at great peril to themselves.

The details of the surrender had been worked out in satisfactory terms to General Crook, Geronimo was to come in next day. But an American at the San Bernardino Ranch, one Tribollet by name, sold whiskey to the Indians. Geronimo and a part of his band got drunker than 700 dollars, high-tailing it back into the Sierra Madre Mountains of Old Mexico, leaving Crook to hold the bag. Badgered by his superiors over the way he had handled the affair, General Crook asked to be relieved of his command and General Miles took over.

When Geronimo surrendered, General Miles had five thousand regular troops and three hundred Indian scouts in the field. There were seventeen warriors in Geronimo's band, nineteen women and children. As a young officer with a fine military record during the War Between the States and later in his campaigns against the Northern Indians, General Miles did not grow in stature when he succeeded General Crook.

The terms of Geronimo's surrender to General Miles have never been clarified. General Miles' controversy with the higher-ups still makes interesting reading. Anxious to get a hot potato off his hands, General Miles shipped Geronimo East at once. As a matter of fact, Geronimo was on his way before the higher-ups in Washington had decided just what to do.

It was General Miles' manner of deporting all the Chiricahuas on the upper reservation that brought his deepest censure. Soldiers like Bourke, Davis, Gatewood and General Crook, to mention only a few, who were sensitive of their word and honor, heartily disapproved.

Four hundred and forty Chiricahuas, among them some Warm Springs Apaches from New Mexico, were being held at Fort Apache as prisoners of war. These Chiricahuas, incidentally, had seen their reservation, deeded in solemn treaty, taken from them and they had been herded to San Carlos. While they had never been disarmed, they were raising livestock and cultivating their little fields. Disliked by the White Mountain Apaches, they were hated and feared by the whites. In July,

General Miles went to Fort Apache for the purpose of working out some plan whereby these Apaches could be removed to a location in the East.

The picture the General painted for them was glowing, to say the least. At his suggestion, Chato and many of the leading men were induced to go back East and see the Great White Father. As General Miles painted his picture, the Great White Father would, no doubt, give them

lands and livestock if the Chiricahuas would only agree to leave Arizona
peacefully and settle further east.

And the Chiricahuas who journeyed East were well received; they
met President Cleveland—the Great White Father—who gave Chato a
large and imposing silver medal. Then the Secretary of War, the Honorable Mr. Endicott, gave him a certificate to carry away. While the
President promised nothing, Chato received the presents as evidence of
good faith. They pleased the simple Chato and set his troubled mind
at rest.

The Apache delegation was still in Washington, however, when
President Cleveland and General Sheridan decided that not only the
delegation in Washington but all the Chiricahuas at Fort Apache should
be sent to Fort Marion, Florida, and held as prisoners of war. General
Miles, notified of this procedure, approved; however, he wired Washington that since the Apache delegation had journeyed East at his suggestion they might take it as a matter of bad faith. Yet he did not want
the delegation back from Washington, in rounding up the Chiricahuas
they might upset his plans.

So Chato and his party were held en route at Carlisle, Pennsylvania,
for five days and over General Miles' protest they were headed West
again. Then, yielding to the General's entreaties, the War Department
had this delegation stopped in Kansas where Chato and the other members were held in confinement for two months at Fort Leavenworth.

In the meantime, General Miles' plan for rounding up the Chiricahuas at Fort Apache went forward without a hitch. To Colonel Wade's
five troops at Fort Apache four other troops were added. When the
Indians came in on ration day, Miles' plans were executed. The Apaches
were disarmed; men, women and children were herded into wagons
under a strong military escort, started to Holbrook, one hundred miles
away, and loaded on the train for Florida.

Apache scouts who had served faithfully under General Crook for
years were rounded up and deported to Florida, too. In this manner our
great and beneficent government finally solved the problem of the Chiricahuas and brought peace to Arizona. Small wonder both officers and
civilians who were sensitive of their honor hung their heads in shame.

The lowest ebb in our dealings with the Chiricahuas was reached,
however, when on September 12th the Secretary of War sent the fol-

lowing telegram to the Commanding General of the Division of the Missouri:

> "You will cause the Apache Indians now at Ft. Leavenworth to be sent under charge of Capt. Dorst, Fourth Cavalry, by the most direct and expeditious route to St. Augustine, Florida, and upon arrival to be turned over to the commanding officer at the post for confinement with other Indian prisoners now there."

Like many of the deported Apache scouts, Chato had been honorably discharged by General Crook and was living peacefully on his little farm when General Miles induced him to go East with the delegation to Washington. Embittered to his dying day as an exile in a foreign land, small wonder Chato was never able to understand why his Great White Father in Washington had given him the beautiful silver medal.

LAND OF SHADOW

IV

OLE INDIAN JIM didn't wear socks but he always wore cowboy boots. We were on day herd together when he took off a boot to remove a sandburr. "Your granddaddy never wore boots," I said. "No," replied Ole Jim. "He wear moccasin." Then, as an afterthought, Jim added: "Your granddaddy an' my granddaddy fight like hell; you an' me pretty good friends, no?"

It was in the early '20's, we were working together at the old Cross S outfit. The outfit ran their cattle on the San Carlos Reservation and Jim was a full-blooded Apache. His number was M.D. 11, his last name was Whitehead and someone with a sense of humor must have named him. Jim was a black Apache and there was not a fleck of gray in his black, straight, coarse hair. Yet his kindly old face was a mass of wrinkles.

He did not know his age; but he remembered the trek when the Rio Verdes were transferred from their Reservation at Camp Verde to San Carlos. Later, when I looked it up, I found the trek was made in 1875.

There had been an escort of soldiers, and in spite of the escort the Verdes had fought amongst themselves on the trail, several were killed and many wounded. "Fight like hell," was Jim's comment, "some Indians no want go San Carlos."

When an Apache speaks English he doesn't always say just what he means. An Apache stopped a friend of mine one day on the mesa below Fort Apache. "Have you seen an old man?" said the Indian. "He's lost, we can't find him for a week."

"Your father?" said my friend.

"No," replied the Apache, "he's my wife's mother."

It was the Apache's mother-in-law he was hunting; she was found dead on the mesa a short time later having been killed by lightning. Jim's talk was never quite that complicated but there were times when what he said was exactly opposite to what he meant.

A census taker had come to the ranch; he was brusque, full of his business and himself. When he left there was probably little difference in his mind between an Apache and his white brother, the cowpuncher.

One of the punchers didn't know where he was born. It was either Texas or New Mexico, the puncher's family was constantly on the move. "Just put down 'wagon'," said the puncher, by way of helping the official counter fill his paper, "that's where Maw told me I was born."

Still another knew his birthplace but he didn't know his age. His parents had died when he was young. "You mean," said the count taker, "that no one knows your age?" "An uncle might know," said the puncher, "but I ain't had no word from him in twenty years. He never bothered to tell me how old I was, reckon he figgered I'd ask if I was interested."

It was easy to see that the census taker had some doubt as to whether he was being taken for a buggy ride and by the time he got to Ole Jim he was in no mood for trifling.

"Want the Indian, too?" said the foreman.

"I want every cowboy at this ranch," he replied brusquely, turning to Ole Jim.

"What's your name, Indian?"

"Jim Whitehead," he replied, giving the counter one of his best smiles.

"Don't try to be funny with me, Indian," said the official counter.

"That's his name," said the foreman; so the counter wrote it down. Of course, Ole Jim didn't know his age but, at least, he tried to be helpful. "You know Old Man Hayes?" said Jim. Mr. Hayes was an old-time Arizona cowman and in his seventies at this time. "Of course, I know him," snapped the counter. Ole Jim's face lighted. "Me know Old Man Hayes," he said, "ever since Old Man Hayes is little boy." At this the foreman interrupted again: "What the Indian means is that Old Man Hayes has knowed him since the Indian was a little boy."

It was too much for the official counter. Later, in telling of the census taker's visit, one of the punchers said: "He left before he even finished Ole Jim's tally an' when he left he was talkin' to hisself."

Ole Jim was a good cowboy. He had that sixth sense about stock that only the real cowboy has. That knack of knowing what a critter would do before the critter knew. Never a bucking-horse rider, he was a good roper and he had worked with wild cattle all his life. He knew when to crowd one, when to give them room. He always caught more than his share of the wild ones and on the drive he was always at the right place at the right time.

There were always certain men in the outfit who resented him simply because he was an Indian. They didn't like "gut-eaters" and didn't hesitate to say so, no matter how many Indians were present. There were some, of course, who had the decency to keep their feelings to themselves. Ole Jim understood.

On the spring and fall roundup, the outfit sometimes worked half a dozen Apache cowboys. Since some of them couldn't or wouldn't speak English, Jim always acted as straw boss or jigger with his red brothers. Jim knew every foot of the range; many white cowboys riding through the roundup didn't. There were always situations that called for tact on the part of the foreman since no white puncher would ever take "pills" (orders) from an Indian.

"Take six men," the foreman would say, "an' take the old Indian with you; he knows the country an' he can tell you where's the best place to drop off your men." Ole Jim was tactful, too. He knew who his friends were and who disliked him. Yet he always kept his own counsel and there was no man, red or white, that Ole Jim Whitehead feared.

When the cook got high-behind for no apparent reason and threatened him with the gonch hook, Ole Jim picked up a shovel and hit the cook over the head. His majesty, Old Slick an' Greasy, was out for some time, too. It was obvious to everyone that Ole Jim was in the right, but, like all Apache dealings with the whites, it was the Indian who got the worst of it; Ole Jim was laid off.

The foreman who was Jim's friend took him to one side and explained the situation: the cattle were all gathered, the roundup would be over in a few days, with a big outfit to feed he couldn't let the cook go until

they'd shipped. Then he hoped to be through with this particular old Slick an' Greasy for all time and Jim could come back to work. Ole Jim understood and held no resentment toward the foreman.

On the way to the shipping pens, the foreman rode to Jim's tepee. It was midnight and they were holding the herd about a mile above Jim's wickiup. The foreman was dead for sleep; he asked Jim for a blanket and if he'd let him sleep for an hour an' then wake him, as he was afraid the cattle might run. It was a big herd and they were wild and spooky. Jim dug up some bedding and the foreman went to sleep under the ramada by the tepee. When he woke, the sun was in his face and Ole Jim was just riding in. "Herd all quiet," said Jim. The old Apache, rather than wake his friend after an hour's sleep, had rode out to the herd and stood guard, himself, for the rest of the night.

When the outfit camped for any length of time in one place, Jim's family joined him, but they always set their tepee some distance from our camp. It was only on rare occasions that any of his family came to our camp and it was only a few personal friends who were ever invited to Jim's wickiup. "You come tonight my camp," he'd say.

His squaw was a cripple and walked with a crutch. Francisco, an old Apache relative, took care of her when Ole Jim wasn't around. Ole Jim was the only Apache I ever knew who waited on his squaw. There was a kindly quality about Ole Jim, his voice was gentle. I never saw him punish or heard him say a cross word to the children. There was a little boy, a little girl and a daughter going to the Indian School at Phoenix. Sometimes I wrote letters for Jim and read her letters to him. I asked him what he thought about his daughter going to school. "Not good," he said. "Learn lots things good for white people; when she come home, mebbe so unhappy."

I'd made a trip to New York and one night in cow camp I told about getting caught in the subway stampede at Times Square during the rush hour. Jim never could get enough of the story. When I came at night to sit with Jim outside his tepee, "Subway," he'd say, "you tell it." Then Jim would repeat it in Apache to his family. The fact that white people were prodded into the cars like cattle evidently appealed to Ole Jim's sense of humor. I'd picked up some Yiddish expressions which Ole Jim promptly appropriated and took pleasure in yelling at me when we were on the drive. "Oi! gevalt," was always his signal to me that Ole Jim needed help.

The way Jim said things, the twist he gave his words, was always amusing. He heard the saying "More business than a hen with one chicken." But when Jim used it, he simply had "more business than one chicken." Punchers, when shoeing a mean horse, have a common expression: "Stand still, you soanso, or I'll knock a — out of you that will ring like a church bell." "Stand still, you soanso," Jim would say, "or I'll knock a church bell out of you."

Jim was cat-whiskered like a Mexican; he was one of the few Apaches I knew who shaved. The others, for the most part, carried tweezers on a thong about their necks and simply pulled their whiskers out.

It was the custom to clean up at shipping time, to whack the beard with the scissors and then finish with a razor. Jim and I both used the same kind of razor, an Enders. I was out of blades and so was Jim. I'd already used the scissors. "No blades," said Jim. "How about him," I said, pointing to an Apache who didn't speak English. Jim turned and spoke straight-faced to the Indian and the Indian, with a poker face, took the buckskin thong from around his neck and handed Jim his tweezers, which Ole Jim gave to me without batting an eye. They didn't laugh out loud but they enjoyed it as they pictured me pulling out one whisker at a time.

I tried one sweat bath with Jim and only one. He and a couple of his friends had built a sweat lodge by the water. It was built in the same manner as their wickiups only this affair wasn't big enough to cuss a cat in. They had heated rocks. We peeled our clothes and got inside. Even before they began to throw water on the hot rocks I was almost suffocated. I stood it for about two minutes before I broke out and hit the creek. This time they laughed out loud; Jim and the other Indians stayed in a long time, chanting some kind of an Apache song.

On the upper Cross S range there was an Indian "post office." To the punchers it was known as Post Office Ridge. It was nothing put a pile of rocks and boulders where the Apaches placed certain sticks when they had a message they wanted to pass along to each other. Different kinds of wood were used and the sticks were often arranged in a peculiar man-

ner. No white puncher I knew had any idea of their meaning, nor was
Ole Jim any help.

Any time we rode by, I'd say, "Any mail for me today?" He always
stopped and took a long look. "No mail for you today." I was a friend but
I was still a white man and what the Apaches "wrote" to each other was
none of my affair. There was only one occasion where he ever made any
comment as to what the sticks might mean. The outfit was moving camp;
Ole Jim and I were punching the remuda down the long ridge and we
had better than a hundred saddle horses.

As usual we stopped for a look at the post office. Just as a matter of
habit, I said, "Any mail for me today, Jim?" He looked at me and
smiled. "Cowboy move camp, when he go mebbe so Indian kill a beef."
Whether Jim read it in the sticks or not, I didn't know, but I knew he
spoke the truth. The Apaches would kill a Cross S beef as soon as we left
that part of the range.

Jim rode for white outfits all his life but he had all the Apache super-
stitions. He believed the medicine man could bring rain. There were certain Apache ceremonies Jim refused to discuss even with his friends. Let
an owl hoot near an Apache wickiup at night and it's even-money they
move in the morning. I knew the Apaches associated the hooting of an
owl with death. "It makes the blood in the throat," said Jim. That was all
he ever told me. Often when he called the Apache cowboys in the morning Jim would give a few low hoots. I think it was done as a gesture to
show his white brothers he was not afraid. But we observed that it was
always breaking light when Jim did it; he never hooted at night.

On one roundup the cattle were to go to Los Angeles and the boss
had planned to take the old Indian with him. Jim had never been out of
Arizona and he often spoke to me of the things he hoped to see on the
coast. Above all, he looked forward to seeing what he called the "boiling
ocean."

But Ole Jim didn't get to make it. He had a leg broken just before the
outfit shipped. We were camped at Seven Mile. The outfit had just
changed horses at noon and all were mounted when a pony "broke in
two." He was pitching in a circle. Jim was riding a jug-head that was
hard to handle and in the melee the pitching horse kicked Jim's tapadero
and it snapped Jim's leg above the ankle. We carried him to his tepee.
There was no way of getting him to town for some time, so that night the

boss and I went over. He gave Jim some aspirin, told him how and when to take it, and we showed old Francisco and Jim's squaw how to put a cold compress on Jim's leg with towels; it would keep the swelling down. They were very grateful.

Later Jim admitted to me he threw the aspirin away and they took off the cold compress, too, as soon as we left the wickiup. But all night long we could hear the racket that came from Jim's tepee. The medicine man came and sang all night. Next morning when I went to the wickiup at daybreak Jim smiled, said he felt pretty good. His leg looked good, too, and was only slightly swollen. Jim never mentioned the trip to California again nor did I ever hear him speak again of the "boiling ocean."

In the '20's, when the reservation was turned back to the Apaches and the white outfits had to move their cattle off, Ole Jim owned a little bunch of cattle but he was often short of ready cash. He often borrowed small sums from me and always paid it back. "Jim needs ten dollars," he'd say, or maybe it was twenty. If I didn't have it, I'd say so. "Jim needs twenty dollars, you get Jim twenty dollars." He took it for granted I'd get it for him and I always managed to dig it up some way. If I happened to be away when he was ready to return it, he'd go to a mutual friend, give him the money and ask him to send it to me. "He'll be back pretty soon an' you can give it to him yourself," the friend would say. But Ole Jim would insist: "Mebbe so Ross needs twenty dollars now!"

Jim had a couple of nicknames for me: the Apache "Iacho," unprintable in English, and Delgadito, which means "the slim one." If there was a third person present, however, he always called me Ross.

We were alone one night outside his tepee. The big flats were in shadow but the moon was beginning to flood the upper mesas with its soft light. Back on the rim, Jim's brother, the coyote, had already started his nightly serenade. Usually our talk was bantering, Jim laughed a lot; but this night he was deadly serious.

"Where you go when you die?" he said suddenly.

"I don't know," I said, somewhat taken back. "Never thought much about it." And I countered, "Where do you intend to go?"

Death is something I had never heard an Apache speak of before. I knew it was customary to burn the tepee and to destroy all the deceased's possessions. I had seen the food placed at the grave for the long journey and often a little corn for making tulapai, a favorite drink. And in those days it was customary to kill the owner's best horse; he should be mounted well for his long ride through the land of shadows. But the final destination?

"What is it like?" I asked. Jim sat for a long time in silence before he spoke.

"All good," he said. "Out there all good. See all my friends, see all my people. Lots of game; lots to eat, never hungry. Lots of tulapai." It was that simple to Ole Jim.

"Guess you won't see any of your white friends there?"

He pondered that one before he spoke. Yes, he would see his white

friends, maybe, for everything out there was good. He named a few cowpunchers he'd like to see and there was a cavalry officer he hoped to see,
too. Jim didn't know his name but this officer had been kind to him when
Jim was a little boy on the Rio Verde.

I tried to add a lighter touch to the conversation. "You know there's
bound to be trouble if the whites and Indians mix. It's always been that
way and old St. Peter will need a stout fence to keep them apart."

"Who St. Pete?" said Jim. As best I could I told him but he was not
impressed by my sketchy description of St. Peter nor of his official duties.
"No fence," said Jim. "Everything good out there. Where you go?" he
asked again.

I couldn't tell him. I said I didn't know. He shook his head. I knew
I had hurt him. "Jim," I said, "my mother's faith is just as strong as
yours. She believes in a hereafter, too, just as you do."

"Your mother know," said Jim, "your mother right. You talk like little boy tonight, no talk like Delgadito. Your mother know."

It has been many years since Ole Jim started on his long ride through the land of shadows. Some of his old cowpuncher friends have taken the long ride, too. If the final destination is as Ole Jim pictured it: those old cowpunchers, his old friends, will drop their reins and sit awhile in the shade with Jim beside his wickiup; and the cavalry officer, who was kind to a little Apache boy on the Rio Verde, will often ride his way.

TULAPAI

V

OLE INDIAN JIM and I were hunting horses. We were dry when we hit Seven Mile water, and as our ponies plunged their dusty muzzles into the little stream, I swung down to take on some myself.

"Wait," said Ole Jim, "mebbe so, good drink pretty soon."

Thinking Jim probably had a small, cold spring in mind close by, I swung aboard again, and when the ponies had watered out Jim led the way to George G's wickiup, about a quarter down the wash.

Like Ole Jim, George was a full-blooded Apache. He was riding fence for the Cross S outfit. George was drowsing in the shade beside his wickiup when Jim and I rode up. At a sign from her lord an' master, his squaw disappeared into the brush behind the tepee only to reappear with a dipper in each hand. One she gave to Ole Jim and the other she handed to me. The dippers had been fashioned from quart tomato cans and both were brimming full.

It wasn't water; it wasn't milk. I looked at Jim, who smiled. "Tulapai," he said. It was then our host spoke up: "George G, he gotte all the time tulapai."

The making of tulapai was a guardhouse offense and strictly against the rules of the reservation. Having seen some of the aftereffects of the tulapai parties, where the Apaches had fought with knives, axes, clubs, besides gouging and pulling hair, I figured it was a potent drink. I was acquainted with tequilla and mescal, that fiery liquor from across the southern border; but it, at least, was always served in jiggers and the can I held of tulapai was brimming full.

I didn't know whether I was being jobbed or not. Both Jim and George were eyeing me expectantly, and after asking Jim to catch my horse if he ran out from under me, I put the bait down. It tasted much like sour buttermilk; it was cool and not at all unpleasant. I waited a moment but the lightning didn't strike.

"I thought your liquor had a kick."

"No eat two, three, four days, drink all time," said Jim, "then you feel 'em."

Later, on our way back with the lost ponies, we stopped at George's camp and in an offhand way I learned how tulapai was made. Corn is thoroughly soaked in water, then put away to sprout; then dried and ground by hand on the metate or grinding stone. Weeds, roots, root bark, seeds and often a dash of loco weed—in fact, any perennial weed or root—is added that may suit the maker's taste. The mess is usually placed in five gallon coaloil cans, water is added and the stuff is boiled for hours. Then the liquid is poured into empty cans and the mash is reground. Again the residue is added to the liquid and the mess reboiled. Then it is set aside to ferment. Twenty-four hours makes it about right for drinking, they said, but they seldom wait that long.

Our host's bar looked like an old-fashioned swill barrel to me. It was still working; the barrel was covered with mosquito netting, for flies buzzed all about the camp, but the netting is not considered essential. Both Jim and George claimed the drink was nutritious and not intoxicating unless taken in large quantities.

Usually a tulapai party was the occasion for a big drunk, although there were some Apache friends of mine who always had their tulapai and never went to the "wild bunch." But it is a potent drink when taken in quantities and those things dormant in an Apache come to the surface.

Ole Jim loved his tulapai. I never saw him "high." But there was a scar on Jim's forehead that always interested me. And it seems that he was interested in my broken nose. It was seldom he ever asked a direct question, but after he'd fished around awhile I told him how it happened. It gave me a chance to ask about Jim's scar.

"Horse fall with you?" I asked. He shook his head and smiled.

"Tulapai party," he said. An Apache had worked Jim over with a club. "Me sleep long time," said Jim, "long time me sleep."

"Anything happen when you woke up?" I asked.

"Cut him leetle bit," says Jim.

That was all he ever said, but later, from one of the older punchers, I learned that when Jim finished with his opponent he could have been packed off in a gunny sack.

Since their tulapai parties often wound up in a grand brawl and sometimes a killing, I always tried to keep away from their camps when the Apaches were drinking. To this day most of them have no love for their white brothers, knowing what they have been subjected to through the years. We can't blame them, either. Given liquor in quantities, things long buried come boiling to the top.

Had I known there was a tulapai party going I'd have kept on down the wash one day, but there was water in the next canyon. I knew there

were a few Apaches camped on the water there but I had no idea of
what I was riding into until I topped out, almost in the camp itself. The
whole outfit, bucks and squaws—and there were many visitors—was
boiling, cock-eyed drunk.

Had I turned and high-tailed it, they would have enjoyed nothing
better than to have dusted me off with a .30-30. All the Apaches have a
sense of humor which, at times, is peculiarly their own. So I rode directly
into the camp. I knew a few of the Indians by sight and as I stepped
down from my horse one big Apache, drunker than seven hundred
dollars, gave me a whack across the shoulders that nearly flattened me.
At the same time he said, "Long time my friend." Everyone laughed; it
was a good joke as far as the Apaches were concerned and I knew it was
all on me.

As soon as I could get straightened up, I measured my Apache friend;
I wanted him to know that I could play in a friendly fashion, too. Saying,
"Long time my friend," I let him have one with everything I had, at
which the Apaches roared again. It was some time before my friend,
who was in a sitting position, got the point; when he did he laughed
louder than anyone. It was he who brought me a gourd of tulapai that
we shared, after I had picked out the dead flies.

Water was what I wanted, but most of all I wanted to be on my
way, as I knew it was only a question of time until another incident
would occur. The whole party—those still on their feet—crowded about
us, laughing and chattering, as the pony and I watered out. They took
the affair as a huge joke.

I've never been able to see much difference between the way an
Apache and his white brother, the cowboy, drink. When an Apache got
hold of a bottle of "boughten liquor" chances are he had paid ten prices
for the stuff. He thinks he has to drink it all at once; if he doesn't, he's
afraid some white man will take it from him.

The Apache will spread his legs and brace himself after he has
uncorked his bottle. It's even money which way he'll fall, either face
down or on his back. If he had been built with four legs like a horse he
might be able to keep his feet. At any rate, he wouldn't fall as quickly.
I've known punchers, too, with plenty of time and nothing on their minds
except their hats, who would drink it just as fast. The only difference I
observed was that they didn't get down as quickly. In one way the Apache

had the best of it, he was apt to lay right where he fell and sleep it off; while his white brother, the puncher, was apt to get himself and friends into a jackpot before the liquor got him down.

Before the noble experiment was tried, liquor was seldom seen on a cow ranch unless a puncher had just come back from town. It was the custom to bring a bottle or two for friends. The drinking was done in town and the puncher often went months between drinks. There were cowboys of my acquaintance who did not drink, but they were the exceptions. During Prohibition there was a still on every range and, as a friend of mine observed, "the bushes was loaded with white mule." It was not uncommon for the whole outfit to go on a bender at the ranch, which sometimes wound up much as a tulapai party will. There was one I recall. I won't mention the spread, but at that time the outfit ran their cattle on the reservation.

The whole outfit, with the exception of the foreman, had gone to town in the ranch truck. He was rudely awakened in the middle of the night, and none too soon—for the puncher who was driving had the idea that he could take the truck right through the door and unload the outfit at their bunks. He'd wrecked the porch and was backing off for a second try at the door when the foreman intervened. "At that," said the foreman, "he damn near done it, too."

Before he joined the party the foreman counted his lambs. "Where's Dick?" he asked.

"Oh, him," said the driver, "he never was the rider he thinks he is; I dumped him a mile back on the road."

Some time later Dick made it in under his own power. It seems this worthy had insisted on riding the hood of the truck and riding it bareback. Every man in the outfit, with the exception of Dick, carried a jug; Dick had broken his when the driver spilled him, and Dick insisted the driver took an unfair advantage in whipping the truck just as he'd hoisted his jug for a drink.

Back at the ranch the party really got under way, and to this day the details are still hazy; who blacked whose eyes still starts an argument, but any reminiscence sounds like hell's delight. All concerned are agreed on one thing, Big Hank was the first man bedded; but his pooch, a wire-haired fox terrier, missed none of the affair. He bit every man who came

within ten feet of where his master slept and when the melee really started, the pooch was everywhere.

Hank, who slept through it all, was the first to wake next morning. Hank had come from Texas where he'd seen the havoc tornadoes play at times, and the sight he saw that morning brought back the puncher's youth. The only things left standing were the side walls and the roof. The furniture was fit for kindling, there was not a pane of glass intact. Only Hank had not been dog-bit; three punchers could not sit on a horse for several days because of where the pooch got in his work.

During Prohibition, Shorty had a little outfit just off the reservation. He had acquired a ten-gallon charred-oak keg and it was only natural that he should want to fill it. On that particular roundup, no matter how the talk would start, it wound up with Shorty's keg, the making and aging of whiskey. There were arguments pro and con. One puncher had heard that on shipboard whiskey aged twice as fast because of the roll of the ship. So it was suggested that once Shorty got the keg filled he take it up on some high point and roll it off.

"You'd lose it in the brush," said a puncher.

"Hell, no," said Shorty. "Any time I turn ole keg off a high point I'll be ridin' the keg myself an' I expect to be with it when we hit the bottom."

One of the punchers in the outfit had done a short hitch for bootlegging when Prohibition first came in. He knew the operation of a still. Shorty said he didn't intend to peddle the stuff, all he wanted was enough to fill his keg. They threw in together as soon as the roundup was over.

Everything was on the quiet, of course, but once the still was set up and going, every puncher within fifty miles just happened by the ranch. Once there, of course, they stayed. The still was in operation night and day, but even at that Shorty couldn't keep ahead of his guests. The oak keg was empty. Since it was shortly after the First World War, and most of the punchers had been in the service, there were mock drills and maneuvers—but "live" ammunition was used.

It so happened that a lone cowboy drifted in one day who didn't drink. He was promptly lined up in a squad that was being put through its paces by an ex-corporal who was punctuating his orders with shots from a .30-30. It finally occurred to the ex-corporal that he had too many men in the squad. He had not yet made his decision as to which one he'd kill when the non-drinking puncher was missed.

It was always suspected that he was the one who did the Paul Revere and took the word to town. The party was in its second week when the officers sent word to break it up. They knew that Shorty wasn't peddling the stuff. Shorty managed to cache a little in the brush but he never got to fill his keg or ride it off some high point during the aging process.

Old Archie, an Apache, walked off a bluff one night and killed himself. He had just left one tulapai party and was heading for another about a mile away. His passing always brings to mind a drawing I once saw in *Ballyhoo*. Two drunks were walking arm in arm right out an open window that was all of twenty stories above the street. "Let's go to Mike's an' get a drink," says one. "This stuff ain't got no kick."

The making of tulapai has always been more or less of a problem on the reservation where distances are great and the materials for making it are usually at hand. At the present time they make a home-brew which gets quicker action and is said to have the kick of a pack mule. The ingredients are bought in town. When the officer on the upper reservation found the squaws were carrying it concealed under their voluminous dresses, he solved the problem, at least temporarily, by having any squaw who was suspected skip the rope.

Apache veterans of the South Pacific, on their return, found they could not be served a glass of beer in town. But it was a simple matter to get hard liquor from certain unscrupulous whites who always charged them ten prices for it. I don't think the percentage of Apaches who drink is any higher than among their white brothers and sisters. Since they are not supposed to drink at all, as wards of a beneficent government, it only follows that when they do drink they are more obvious. And, as I said before, I've never been able to see much difference between the way an Apache and his white brother handle it, either.

At the old Cross S outfit, one of the punchers "got down" after a trip to town. His bed was on the porch and at the end of two days he had

recovered sufficiently to be able to crawl off the porch on all fours. He
had crawled into the yard when a hound pup joined him and began
chewing grass. It was when the pup gagged that the puncher became
conscious of his compadre's presence; he rolled a sympathetic eye in the
hound pup's direction. "You pore soanso," he said. "So you been to
town, too!"

The late Charlie Russell, who drew and painted the Plains Indians
better than any other white man, to my way of thinking, told me this
yarn a long time ago about a cowpuncher friend of his. "An Indian will
do anything for whiskey," said the puncher. "An Indian spotted a couple
of quarts I had in my saddle-bags. He keeps biddin' higher an' higher.
The booze I got ain't worth over four dollars but he finally offers me the
horse he's ridin'; it's a good horse, too, an' easy worth a hundred."

"You traded?" says Charlie.

"Hell, no!" replied the puncher. "It's all the booze I got."

THE WILD BUNCH

VI

JOE and I were on wrangle; it was just light enough to see a horse when he jumped the wild bunch out. I could hear them coming down the ridge long before they came in sight; but as they thundered past me down the long ridge for a moment they were in silhouette against a morning sky. The stud was in the lead, his long mane and tail were streaming in the wind. There must have been all of fifty in the bunch and I caught a fleeting glimpse of one of our pack mules. It was two years before the outfit got him back.

They were out of sight when they hit the pasture fence—but the sound was sickening. Then I heard a wild one scream. It might have been the one still struggling in the wire when Joe and I rode up. As she struggled, torn and bleeding, in the wire Joe put a merciful slug between her eyes. Then he and I fixed fence, rounded up our saddle horses and headed back for the ranch.

It was at the old Bar F Bar outfit, thirty years ago. The outfit ran most of their cattle on the reservation. The Apaches, working horses, had run the wild bunch through the pasture fence the day before.

It was estimated there were five thousand wild horses on the Bar F Bar range alone. They ran in bands, each wild stud having his own bunch of mares. It depended on how much of a fighter he was as to how big a bunch he had. It was seldom a wild one would weigh nine hundred pounds. They were never the beautiful creatures posing on some high point that are so commonly seen in the movies. The old studs were always battle-scarred, and the day always came when some younger and stronger stud whipped the old boy, ran him off and appropriated his band.

Some of the fights for supremacy were deadly affairs. But usually the stud left and left in a hurry after he was whipped. Hunting saddle horses on Mescal, I witnessed one affair. I had the wind on the bunch and through the glasses it was like having a ringside seat and the wind brought me all the sounds of battle.

The old stud was a bay and battle-scarred. There must have been all of forty mares and colts in his band. He had rounded up his mares ready to break them into flight. I thought he must have winded me, when I saw the young buckskin coming toward him up the mesa.

The buckskin had four mares and two little colts in the band. The mares were trailing the stud at some distance and seemed bored with the whole affair. But the buckskin meant business. Tossing his black mane in the wind, he trumpeted his challenge when he was still a good two hundred yards away; and while he wheeled and trotted in a half circle, his approach was steady. The old bay stud was going through the same maneuvers, wheeling in circles and trumpeting as he answered the buckskin's challenge.

The buckskin was within fifty yards of the old bay and they were circling each other like boxers, but all the time the circle was growing smaller. Then, suddenly, the old bay struck and the buckskin went to his knees, but he was on his feet in an instant. Then they were both on their hind feet, snapping at the throat. The next moment they had wheeled away and were planting well-placed kicks. They feinted and blocked like boxers. As they snapped and struck for each other's throats, their popping teeth cracked like pistol shots.

The mares and colts were gathered in a great half-circle now, watching the fight. There was no sign of excitement among them. Occasionally

a little colt, as if suddenly aware of the affair, left the band to investigate but he was promptly put back by his mother.

As the fight wore on it was easy to see that the old bay stud was tiring, though the old boy knew every trick. But the buckskin, the aggressor, always kept coming in. Both studs were glistening with sweat. As the sunlight struck the buckskin, he looked like burnished gold and blood was flowing from his shoulder where the old bay stud had struck.

As the fight wore on, even the sounds of battle that floated to me down the wind were changed; the studs no longer trumpeted. There were grunts and squeals of rage. Then suddenly it was over. The old bay turned and ran. The buckskin did not follow but he trumpeted long and loud. And rounding up both bands of mares he headed them toward the water, nipping the flank of any mare he thought was a trifle too slow. At intervals he wheeled and tossed his head and the wind brought me his challenge.

A few days later two of us happened onto the body of the old bay stud less than a half mile from the scene of the fight. His old neck and withers were covered with scars that told of his battles over the years. At first glance he didn't seem to have been badly hurt, at least not enough to have caused his death. But on looking closer we found it, the death wound in his throat.

Nor was the victory always to the strong. The outfit owned a brown stud that would weigh eleven hundred pounds and there were about forty picked mares in his band. They ran in the R. S. pasture. We found the brown stud alone one day. He had been whipped; his opponent had done a good job of it, too. The stud was taken to the ranch and doctored for several days; later we found the mares and the stud who had whipped the brown and appropriated his band. It was a little Indian stud who wouldn't have weighed eight hundred pounds had he been soaking wet.

Since there were as many wild horses on the range as cattle, the wild ones were a problem. Most of the punchers carried .30-30 saddle guns, with orders to kill a wild one at every opportunity—with the understanding, of course, that the Apaches were not to find it out. And there were strict orders not to catch the wild ones, but for the most part both orders were ignored. Most cowpunchers are horse lovers and would not kill a wild one unless it was necessary, and since the Old Man spent most of his time in town they caught a wild one at every opportunity.

It was a country of mesas, deep canyons and the long ridges; knowing the country, a rider on a good horse had every advantage. A rider would wait along a long ridge while another puncher put the wild bunch out past him. On a good horse, a good roper could usually get a throw at the one he wanted. As for excitement, it was more fun than running wild cattle. And running wild horses often became an obsession. There was one man in the outfit we'll call Steve. He would quit the cattle any time to catch a wild one. As a matter of fact, he caught and led out so many wild ones he was finally barred from working on the reservation. Steve never bothered with a bill of sale.

Steve and I were at the holdup one day; a band of wild horses had balled up the drive. Cattle coming down had started to rim out and turn back as the wild bunch went racing through them. The first cattle had started to filter into the narrow canyon where we were holding up when I missed Steve. The boys on the outside circle were in before he showed up but I knew from the gleam in his eye what had happened. The fact that we had lost half the cattle didn't bother him, either. He had caught a wild horse an' tied him down!

Later, when we went over to see what he had caught, Steve, waxing eloquent about the wild one's points, got careless and the wild one, although tied down, reached out and took a good-sized piece out of the calf

of Steve's leg. "That thing is loco," said a puncher. Steve insisted he was a good horse, though he later admitted the puncher was partly right.

He was riding this pony he had caught on the drive one day when the pony went to pitching. It was rim-rock country. Steve tried to turn him and couldn't but Steve stepped off before the pony pitched over the bluff. The rim was better than twenty feet high and Steve, taking it for granted the pony had killed himself, crawled down to get his saddle. But the pony was on his feet, unharmed and grazing contentedly. "Only one thing wrong with him," said Steve, "he just don't give a damn!"

Most of the punchers usually dickered with the Indians; any Apache

on the reservation who owned a brand could give a bill of sale. And the procedure was simple. First catch the horse and then contact an Indian. It went about as follows:

Puncher: "I saw a sorrel on Mescal the other day with two white stockings; he's pretty wild, don't know whether I can catch him or not but I'll give you four dollars for a bill of sale an' take a chance." Often a bill of sale was as low as two dollars and never over ten. But one thing was certain, the puncher always had the pony before any money was put out.

The stud usually stood guard until his band had watered out. He was always on the lookout for riders. It was he who rounded up his band and broke them into flight at the first sign of danger. If riders were in the country, the wild ones often became frantic for water and even the stud grew careless.

Since the horse wrangler always rides the sorriest horses in the outfit, it was seldom I ever got a chance at a good one. Old Ed Hill and I were packing salt when we trapped a bunch on the water. We had the wind on them that day and, the way the canyon boxed up, the wild ones had to pass close enough for a throw as they came out.

It was the stud who came out first and he came with a rush. I made a lucky throw but I caught him too deep in the shoulders. With the rope tied hard and fast to the saddle horn, something was bound to happen and it did. The cinch broke and for an instant I had a bird's-eye view of what was going on below—it was a mad scramble, too, as the mares and colts came out. But it was only for an instant. I was still in the saddle when the stud took off and that ride through the rocks and boulders will be long remembered. Old Ed was laughing; it was a wonder he caught the horse as we came out past him.

I wanted to lead the wild one in but Ed said no. "He ain't worth two bits at best an' you know what the orders is." Ed always packed a .30-30 but he was a horse lover, too, so we turned the wild one loose. That night in camp the picture Old Ed gave of the affair was vivid, to say the least. "When the cinch broke, with them bat-winged leggin's floppin', he looked for all the world like a turkey buzzard takin' off."

Every time the outfit moved camp, two men went on ahead to run the wild ones out. When a gentle saddle horse got with the band, it often took the whole outfit and the dog to catch him. All geldings love a little colt. Usually a stud would whip a saddle horse out of the band. But often through the glasses I have observed one of our gentle saddle horses, gone to the wild bunch, giving care and affection to some spindly-legged colt.

A mockey (wild mare) will seldom go back after her colt that could not keep up in the wild flight that led to safety. Often a little colt who had been left behind would find our saddle horses and come in with the remuda in the morning, and it was not uncommon to ride up on a little colt who had been left behind. The outfit, always on the move, had no way of caring for them. Left alone, if the coyotes didn't pull them down, they starved to death. It was never easy to put a .45 slug between their eyes

but it was more humane. A little colt is nothing but a horse in miniature. As the little fellow would look at a rider with his eyes shining—well, it's something a rider won't forget.

Always I have preferred horses to cattle. History tells us that Cortes brought the first horses to this continent in 1519, eleven stallions and five mares of Arabian stock. When De Soto landed on the coast of Florida he also brought horses with him. It is highly probable that some of Cortes' and De Soto's horses escaped and—some place on the great plains—the bands were joined. For when Zebulon Pike made his trek west in 1806, the plains were teeming with wild horses, descendants of Cortes' and De Soto's bands. In the Blackfoot tribe in Montana there are a couple of pieces of Spanish armor that the Plains Indians took back as souvenirs when they came afoot to the great Southwest in their quest of horses. And it was the horse who changed an entire way of life on this continent.

The Apaches may have been some of the first Indians mounted. Yet among cowboys they are not considered as good horsemen even to this day. And an Apache wild horse hunt was really something to behold.

They would meet at a designated spot and make their drive. The holdup was usually one of the natural corrals. Always an individualist, each Apache was strictly on his own and acted accordingly. It was not uncommon to have a big bunch of wild ones trapped, when here would come an old buck—going over and under with the double of his rope— in pursuit of some old mare and colt. He would not only come into the holdup on the dead run but go right on through and the next instant the wild ones would be scattered from hell to breakfast, with every Apache kicking his horse in the belly in pursuit of a pony he wanted.

The quickest way to gentle a wild one is to feed him. During the middle '20's, a movie outfit took a wild horse picture in Arizona. They paid a dollar a head for every wild horse brought in and the punchers gathered over a thousand head that were fed for a week in a big corral. Then the day came for the big scene, the stampede. In some manner, two Shetland ponies had got mixed with the band and when the stampede was started these two Shetlands came out in the lead. That day the director was the wildest thing on the reservation.

Some of the best horses in the Bar F Bar remuda were Indian ponies. While undersized, they had big hearts and their endurance was remarkable. Raised in the rough country, they were agile as cats among the rocks and boulders. Grain was not fed on the roundup in those days, the ponies rustled. Most punchers prefer a bigger horse. But it was my observation that, given the same amount of work, it was the ponies, the ones raised in the country, who came through the roundup in the best shape.

Many of the ponies I speak of came from the wild bunch and they were the tops, of course. Over the years, with the best blood of the range

cut out, most of the wild horses have no commercial value except as fertilizer, dog and chicken feed.

Every excuse has been used to get rid of them. Stockmen say the wild horses eat too much grass, drink too much water. On the reservation, dourine, a horse disease, was the excuse and they were exterminated. Over ten thousand wild horses were shot and killed on the reservation in the early '30's. Old saddle horses and pack mules from the white outfits, gone to the wild bunch, were exterminated, too. The government paid so much a head for each branded animal killed. The Apaches protested. The Apache usually prefers a horse to a cow in spite of the difference in their commercial value.

A friend, a horse lover, saw the last of the wild ones to be killed on the reservation at Ash Flat. For days, weeks and months the killing had gone on. There wasn't a dozen left in the bunch and they were half-starved, but when the hunters jumped them out that morning they came

across the big flats, running like the wind. Then the guns opened and one
after another they went down. They were underfed and undersized. In
many instances the hoofs were gone. But there was nothing wrong with
their hearts. They had made their last run on bloody, spongy stumps.

APACHE KID

VII

WHEN the old Apache and his two squaws moved in on the water and set up their wickiup about a hundred yards below Uncle Mac Robinson's line camp, it was an ideal arrangement as far as the Indians were concerned; Uncle Mac killed a beef at regular intervals. Since he always divided with his red brothers, other Apaches moved in and—but for an unexpected incident—the Indian camp gave promise of becoming a growing and permanent affair.

Uncle Mac was alone in the line camp and it was dark when he heard the three shots from the rim. He figured a puncher was trying to locate his camp and his surmise was right. Not long after he replied to the shots a cowboy came riding in.

The puncher, a new hand, was none too certain of the line camp's location. He brought a note from the foreman, stayed all night at the camp but he pulled out long before daybreak next morning. It was hardly good daylight when an old buck walked into Mac's camp. He studied the ground intently before he spoke. "Cowboy come last night?" Uncle Mac shook his head. The old Apache looked long at the tracks on the ground before he spoke again: "Cowboy come last night?"

"Cowboy no come last night," said Uncle Mac who was always ready to have his fun. Lowering his voice, he said in all seriousness: "My friend, the Kid, come last night; I feed the Kid."

When Uncle Mac got in from his day's ride that evening, the Apache camp was deserted. The Indians had moved en masse, such was their fear of the Apache Kid.

Kid, a full-blooded Apache, was the most dreaded and feared of all the renegades who ranged through Arizona and New Mexico during the late '80's and the early '90's. Trailed and hunted by the U. S. Cavalry, sheriffs' posses and Apache scouts, he eluded them all. He was even more vindictive against his own people than against the whites. For without the aid of Apache scouts, the soldiers and civilians who hunted him were helpless on his trail. He ranged from the Sierra Madre Mountains in Old Mexico to the White River Agency in Arizona. And aside from his own clan of blood relatives, he killed everyone who stood in his way.

Kid had married a daughter of Eskiminzin, the Aravaipa chief, and he took no other woman until misfortune befell him. Nor was the woman Kid loved allowed to accompany him on the trail. Kid had not always been an outlaw; for years he was a trusted scout and he was top sergeant of the company when his great trouble came.

Ski-Be-Nan-Ted was his Apache name. When he was in his early teens his father set up his wickiup in the hills above the little mining camp at Globe. This was in 1876. Since Apache names have always been more than a mouthful, the Apache boy was simply called "Kid," and because he would work he became well known in the little mining camp. In many respects he seemed to prefer the white man's way; he spoke good English, had many friends among the whites, was courteous and agreeable.

He worked for various cow outfits in the district, herding beef; and he was in his late teens when Al Sieber, chief of Apache scouts, enlisted Kid in his company.

Kid was with Sieber at the Battle of the Big Dry Wash. He was with Sieber when Sieber went to Mexico with General Crook after Geronimo and the other hostiles in 1883. Kid was in the scouts when that gallant soldier Captain Emmet Crawford was killed in Mexico, in 1886, by Mexican irregulars while in pursuit of hostile Apaches. He was top sergeant of his company in 1888 and placed in full charge of the scouts when Sieber left to accompany Captain Pierce, the agent, on a trip to White River which was at that time a sub-agency of the San Carlos Reservation.

There are two versions as to how Kid's trouble befell him. Both Dan Williamson and Bill Sparks knew Kid, and since I knew and respected both Williamson and Sparks, I give each version although they were agreed that it was liquor that caused Kid trouble.

According to Williamson, Kid's father, who was then camped not far from the agency, gave a big dance. Tulapai, Apache liquor, was plentiful and the affair wound up in a big drunk. Next morning Kid's father was found dead in his wickiup, stabbed through the heart. Suspicion· pointed to an Apache named Rip. Since it was Apache custom for the oldest son to exact vengeance, Kid, when he was sent by Sieber to arrest Rip, killed him. Kid then rode to his own camp, got drunk and sent word to Sieber that he wanted to see him. Sieber ordered him to come in, and when Kid with some of his scouts rode to Sieber's tent, they were drunk.

Sparks says that as soon as Captain Pierce and Sieber left for the White River sub-agency, a camp of Apaches up the river began brewing tulapai and when Sergeant Kid and his men rode to the camp, they joined the party instead of destroying the liquor and arresting the culprits as their standing orders required. The party lasted better than a week. An Indian was killed, and while Kid and his men had nothing to do with the killing, they were in no condition to arrest the murderers. Sieber and Captain Pierce had just returned when Kid and his men, still drunk, rode to Sieber's tent at the agency.

At Sieber's request, Kid handed him his rifle and disarmed the rest of his men. Sieber then ordered Kid to take his men to the guard house, order the Sergeant of the guard to lock them up, himself included. But in a few minutes they returned to Sieber's tent. In some manner, the drunken scouts had secured guns and ammunition and they began firing into the air. As Sieber reached for a rifle in his tent to quell the disturbance, he was shot in the ankle; during the excitement that followed, Kid and his men escaped.

In a few weeks they had been driven into the agency by the troops. Kid and his men surrendered, were tried and sentenced for mutiny and were given long terms in a Federal prison. They had served a few months when they were pardoned by President Cleveland.

Sieber, who spent a year in bed with his wound and was crippled for life, was very bitter. And though witnesses testified that Kid did not fire the shot that struck him, he was especially bitter towards Kid whom he

blamed for the whole affair. On Sieber's insistence, Kid and his men were tried in a civil court at Globe, and on October 25, 1889, were sentenced to serve seven years each in the territorial prison at Yuma.

The first big leg of their journey from Globe to Yuma was by Concord stage. The first stop was at Riverside station, about forty miles from Globe, where the party spent the night. Eugene Middleton, the driver, routed them out early next morning and they were on their way long before daybreak.

Glen Reynolds, the sheriff of Gila County, and Hunky-dory Holmes, a deputy, were in charge of the prisoners. Accounts vary as to their number. There may have been as many as eight. And while many of the Apache prisoners, other than Kid's men, had received longer sentences for more serious crimes, only Kid and two of his men wore leg irons and handcuffs. The rest of the Apaches were simply handcuffed, and there was one Jesus Avott, a young Mexican sentenced to two years for stealing a pony, who wore no irons whatsoever.

Sheriff Reynolds, who had ridden horseback the first day, left his horse at the station and rode on the box with Middleton, the driver. Holmes, the deputy, rode in the stage with the prisoners as he had on the previous day. Both men wore heavy overcoats over their gun belts and six-shooters since the morning was cold. Reynolds carried a shotgun. His deputy carried a Winchester rifle. Both the sheriff and his deputy fired their guns repeatedly and were said to be in an exuberant mood that morning, a mood not caused by the crisp morning air.

After leaving the station, the road wound through a sandy wash for some distance. When the overloaded stage reached the steep, winding hill, Middleton suggested that all the party, except Kid and his two men who wore leg irons, walk up the hill. When Middleton started the team, the Mexican, Jesus Avott, was walking directly behind the stage. Sheriff Reynolds followed in the lead of the Apache prisoners, Deputy Holmes brought up the rear.

As the stage lurched up the steep, winding grade, Middleton heard a shot but thought nothing of it. He had stopped the stage to let the horses blow when an Apache prisoner covered him with Holmes' rifle, firing almost instantly. Middleton fell from the seat to the ground with a bullet through his neck, and although he was paralyzed from the shock for some time, he did not lose consciousness.

While there was evidently no prearranged plan of escape, the Apaches had been quick to take advantage of the situation. As the party walked up the hill, the prisoners narrowed the distance between themselves and the sheriff, while others dropped back; the sheriff and his deputy were attacked at the same instant.

The sheriff was still struggling with his assailants when he was killed by a shot from the rifle the Apaches had wrested from Holmes. A strange fact developed at the inquest: while Sheriff Reynolds had been shot through the heart, there were no wounds on the deputy's body; Holmes had died of a heart attack during the struggle.

The Mexican, Jesus Avott, was not molested by the Apaches. Unhooking and mounting one of the lead horses, he was bucked off three times. After his third attempt, the Mexican gave it up and went afoot several miles to the nearest ranch for help. For his part in the affair he was pardoned.

Both the sheriff and his deputy were stripped of their arms and ammunition. The sheriff's watch and considerable money was taken from his pockets. The keys for the handcuffs and shackles were taken, and after Kid and his two companions were released, the whole group came and stood about Middleton. They were evidently speculating about his wound. One of the Indians picked a large, jagged rock and was about to crush his skull when Kid intervened, even to the point of seizing the Apache's arm. They spoke in Apache for some time, and after stripping Middleton of his overcoat, they left.

Middleton recovered from his wound and told me, years afterward, he always believed Kid saved his life. With the killing of Sheriff Reynolds and Deputy Holmes, one of the greatest manhunts in the history of the Southwest was begun and it was to last for more than five years.

With U. S. Cavalry, sheriff's posses and Apache scouts on their trail,

the outlaws made their escape into the Sierra Madres in Old Mexico.

It was only a few months until a white man was murdered by three Apaches in the Sierra Ancha Mountains in Arizona. Henry Thompson, succeeding Glen Reynolds as sheriff of Gila County, trailed the three killers to a camp near Fort Apache and arrested one man. The killers were positively identified as not of Kid's band. Sieber, however, also investigated; he claimed that Kid and two of his men were the killers. Since Sieber was a government scout and backed by the military, Sheriff Thompson was forced to release his prisoner, much against his will.

When Kid found himself accused of nearly every crime committed in the Territory, with a reward of $5,000 on his head he grew vindictive; especially so toward his own people, since Apache scouts who had been his friends and had served under him now took his trail. He became the acknowledged leader of all the renegade Apaches who raided out of the Sierra Madres in Old Mexico; though Kid, himself, was a lone wolf, seldom taking more than one or two men. Often, in his raids on the reservation, Kid was alone.

There were many renegade Apaches who did not come in when Geronimo surrendered to General Miles at Skeleton Canyon, Arizona, in 1886, but stayed in Old Mexico. There was one warrior, named Massey, who later became one of Kid's men; in craft and cunning he was equaled only by Kid.

Massey was one of the many Chiricahuas who were shipped to Florida from Arizona before Geronimo's deportation. At some place east of the Mississippi River he escaped from the train. Traveling by night and hiding by day, it was months before he reached his homeland. During his long journey and after his return, no white man is known to have seen his face. Like Kid, but for some unknown reason, he was even more bitter toward his own people than the whites.

It will never be known just how many white men Kid killed in the more than five years that he was hunted. But there was positive proof that Kid killed Nat Whitman, an old scout, on Blue River and took food and ammunition from his cabin.

One of Kid's men told a squaw, whom he had allowed to return to the reservation, of Kid's part in the killing of two cowboys near Wilcox. Apache scouts and the cavalry had been on his trail for days. Kid and his man were afoot and had killed a cow. They were cutting meat from the dead animal when three cowboys rode up to investigate. Hiding behind the carcass, the Apaches killed two of the punchers while the third escaped.

Kid and his companion killed two ranchers in the Sulphur Springs valley a short time later to get horses. Again there was definite proof that

Kid and one of his men killed two cowmen on their way to the roundup between Bonita and Eagle Creek. The scouts and cavalry were close to Kid's trail at the time. They came upon the bodies of the two dead cowmen, but the fresh horses Kid and his man had taken allowed them to outdistance their pursuers.

While Captain, later Colonel, Emelio Kosterlitsky and his Mexican rurales were trailing a party of Mexican smugglers who had crossed from the American line into Sonora, they rode up on their dead bodies; the smugglers had been ambushed, to a man had been wiped out by the Apaches. Taking the Indians' trail, rurales killed three Apaches in a running fight and Captain Kosterlitsky found a watch, with Sheriff Reynolds' name engraved on the case, on one of the Indians. The watch was returned to Reynolds' widow in Globe, Arizona. Kid may or may not have been with this band.

One after another the Apaches who killed Sheriff Reynolds and Deputy Holmes were tracked down and killed. Kid seemed to bear a charmed life. Often for months at a time he rested in the fastness of the Sierra Madre range in Old Mexico. But it was never long before he

raided the reservation again, and his raids struck terror into the heart of the Apaches.

With the cavalry on his trail for the killing of a white man in New Mexico, Kid stole a squaw from the reservation only a few miles from the San Carlos Agency. As the family sat in their wickiup, Kid suddenly appeared and seizing one of the daughters dragged her from the wickiup before the eyes of her astonished family. When the addled father collected his wits and pursued with a rifle, Kid shot him through the heart.

At sound of the shot all the Apaches in the little village came boiling from their tepees. During the excitement, the girl escaped and Kid disappeared in the brush. Soldiers and Apache scouts came from the agency and took up the trail that led nowhere. Shortly after dark, Kid crawled down from his hiding place in a large cottonwood tree, stole another squaw from a nearby tepee and made good his escape.

Some of the squaws Kid killed when they were too worn out to accompany him on the trail, others he allowed to return to the reservation. And there is one of his squaws living on the reservation today who was stolen when a young girl.

Nor were the Apache scouts above giving Kid a wide berth when occasion offered. Jimmie Gibson, an old-time Arizona cowpuncher, had some horses he wanted that ran on the Tables, on the south side of the Gila River. Jimmie was riding down one of the long ridges near the old Bar F Bar headquarters when two Apache scouts rose from their hiding place in the brush. "Where you go?" they asked. Jimmie stated his mission. "No go tonight," said the scouts. "Kid camp at Mud Springs tonight."

Since they were a good five miles from the Springs and went no closer that night, Jimmie figured they didn't want Kid any too badly. Jimmie camped with the scouts and rode with them to Mud Springs late next morning; the scouts gave Kid ample time to be on his way. At Mud Springs the sign showed where an Apache and a squaw had camped the night before.

Jimmie knew Kid; years ago when we were together at the Cross S outfit he told me how on one occasion he could easily have killed Kid and claimed the reward. Jimmie was range-branding on the Wine Glass range at the time. He was in a thicket, having just branded a yearling maverick and turned it loose, when he observed an Apache and squaw coming his way. They were riding double on a pony and had no inkling of his presence. Jimmie promptly put out his little branding fire. In those days, all cowpunchers rode with a sharp eye. When Jimmie recognized the Apache as Kid, he pulled his rifle from the saddle boot and pumped a shell into the barrel. "Five thousand reward," said Jimmie, "dead or alive, an' me workin' for wages at the time. Kid and his squaw passed within forty yards of where I was hid in the thicket, holding my pony's nose so he wouldn't nicker. I could have used five thousand dollars, too, but I never wanted that kind of money."

Cline's outfit was working in the Four Peaks country and they were camped at the troughs, high on the east side of the range. They were range-branding and Hardy Shell, a puncher, was on his way to camp when a voice called to him, in good English, to "come on down." Not recognizing the voice and unable to see who was calling him, Shell rode on into camp.

Late that evening, Sheriff Thompson of Gila County rode into camp. Kid had killed a white man in Reno Pass the day before and the sheriff was on his trail. Without doubt it was Kid, wanting a horse, who had

called to the cowboy. Next morning the sheriff and the cowboys trailed
Kid for several miles up Salome Creek but Kid escaped.

Wid Childers, a friend, was once dismounted by Kid when Wid was
on the roundup. Wid and a Mexican cowboy were on their way to camp

when Kid appeared out of the brush with a rifle in his hands and told
Wid to get down.

"Isn't that Old Man ——'s horse?" said Kid as he looked at the
brand. "Well, tell the Old Man I took his horse. I used to work for him."

About this time another armed Apache appeared and Kid ordered
the Mexican to dismount, saying he wanted his horse, too. The Mexican
began to protest, not knowing who Kid was; Wid had dismounted and
was on tenderhooks, he told the Mexican to dismount and do it pronto.
Wid said he didn't enjoy the walk to camp and that he felt rather foolish

about the affair until he met a troop of cavalry pounding up the canyon on Kid's trail.

Unlike Massey's, the manner of Kid's passing is unknown to this day. Old Massey had been ill for months, too ill to walk, and he was dying when he allowed the last squaw he had stolen to return to her people on the reservation. He, too, had killed other squaws lest they betray his hideouts to the Apache scouts. Now it made no difference.

An old-timer who had known Kid claimed to have seen him among Villa's troops on the border as late as 1915. But when Walapai Clark killed one of Kid's squaws in the Galiuro Mountains, Kid's raids on the reservation ceased. Clark had hobbled out some horses not far from his cabin. When he went at dusk to throw them together again, he saw an Indian moving toward the horses. Slipping back to his cabin, Clark got his rifle and waited along the trail. It was dark when two Indians passed in silhouette against the sky and Clark opened fire. The next morning Clark found he had killed a squaw, identified as one Kid had stolen from the reservation. The other Indian was wounded; Clark followed the bloody trail for some distance when it disappeared.

The reward for Kid was never claimed and was finally withdrawn by the Territory. The manner of Kid's passing will always be a mystery.

SIEBER

VIII

I HELPED Dad feed the horses. When we finished he went to the cabin to wash up before supper an' I went down to my corral to have a look at my stock. I'd built the little corral myself an' while my mount were only stick horses, they were just as real to me as any horse Dad had in his string. Of course, they were named after Dad's horses. Chappo was my top horse, he was short-coupled with a big barrel. He could go all day an' all night. Dad said in all his life he'd never rode a horse with a bigger heart.

I'd just decided to move Chappo—Blaze was pretty bad about kicking—when I looked up an' saw them coming.

They were Apaches, bucks, too. Each one of them had a rag tied round his head. They wore clouts an' long moccasins that come almost to their knees. I only took one quick look but I saw the rifles, too, an' they were heading up the trail in single file towards the cabin.

"Apaches!" I yelled. "Apaches!" Dad heard me. I don't remember mounting Chappo but I was riding a stick horse when I busted into the cabin. Mother's face was white. Dad was standing behind the half-closed door with his Henry rifle at full cock. I was no more than inside the cabin when I heard Dad speak: "It's all right, Mary," he says, "it's all right— it's Al Sieber an' his scouts."

While Dad was speaking he let the hammer down on his rifle, stood it behind the door, an' walked outside the cabin.

After Sieber and Dad shook hands, Sieber turned an' said something to his scouts in Apache. I didn't know what he said but the Apaches scattered out all about the place. In no time, even before Sieber finished washing up, they had little fires going. Dad went to the north side of the cabin, unrolled the meat tarp and took them a whole quarter of beef; it was a hind-quarter, too. Dad wasn't afraid of the Apaches no more than Sieber was.

Mother had supper almost ready, but Dad took down the jug that stood on the fireplace. It was out of my reach, same as his rifle that he kept on the two pegs above the fireplace.

Dad didn't like Apaches but he liked Sieber. Later, Mother told me they had fought on opposite sides during the Civil War, but Dad liked him even if Sieber was a Yankee. When Dad says, "There never was an Apache who was any damn good," Sieber shook his head. "They're not much different from whites," he says, "just raised different. There's always the good an' the bad."

Dad didn't say any more about the Apaches, but after Mother cleared the dishes he got the jug down again an' set it on the table. Dad an' Sieber both laughed a lot. But when Dad told him how I come bustin' into the cabin on Chappo, my top horse, Sieber didn't laugh.

"Where is the horse?" he says. An' when I brought Chappo out of my room in the lean-to, Sieber said he was a fine horse. I liked Sieber so I went an' got the rifle I'd made from soft pine. "It's a Henry," I says, "like Dad's." Sieber said it was a fine rifle, too, an' when he spread his big hands for me I went an' sat on his lap.

Sieber had stood his rifle behind the door when he came into the cabin and he had hung his cartridge belt with his six-shooter an' knife on one of the pegs above the fireplace. He put me down long enough to take his knife from the belt an' to pick up a piece of soft pine by the fireplace. I didn't pay much attention at first, just thought he was whittling. It was nice to set in his lap an' listen while he an' Dad talked. It wasn't until he took his six-shooter out of the belt an' laid it on the floor in front of him that I knew what he was up to. All the time he was talking to Dad, he was carving me a six-shooter just like his own. It was exactly the same length, too, a big one, because I saw him measure it.

"Now, Johnnie, you're fixed," he says. "You've got a good mount of horses, a Henry rifle an' a Colt .45 six-shooter—enough for any cowboy! Or, mebbe, you'd like to be a scout?" I'd always intended to be a cowboy like Dad, never had thought about anything else until Sieber came that night.

I was still awake when Sieber went out. Dad an' Mother both asked him to sleep in the lean-to with me. I hoped so, too, but he slept with the Apaches. I was watching from the window when he went out, he was even bigger than Dad. He carried his belt with his knife an' six-shooter in the crook of his left arm. He carried his rifle in his right hand, he limped a little as he walked. I watched him spread his blankets by one of the little fires. There were Apaches all about him.

I must have gone to sleep for when I looked out next time it was dark, the moon was down. The little fires were dead. Sieber and his Apache scouts were gone.

Mother didn't like Apaches any more than Dad. She wouldn't let one in the house, yet she fed them when they came. Dad wouldn't let a buck light on the place. Any time a buck rode up an' Dad was home, he put him on his way; told him he'd unload him in the yard for keeps if he didn't pull his freight. I guess they understood Dad, too, it was seldom that they came. Dad didn't like it, either, when Mother fed the kids an' squaws. He said it was bad enough to have them living on our beef without coming to the house.

Dad didn't even like the Apache scouts that Sieber had with him. He said that Sieber trusted them too far. I knew Dad must be right. I played Sieber now almost as much as I punched cows but I always kept my scouts in line, never trusted none of them.

We didn't have much company except a cowboy now an' then. I was down in my corral when a stranger rode in one day. He was a white man an' rode a mule. I knew he wasn't a cowboy from the funny clothes he wore, an' he didn't carry a rope. Instead of a rifle in the saddle boot, there was a shotgun slung to the pommel. He carried two wild turkeys that were slung behind his saddle. I looked just long enough to take him in an' the stranger never saw me when I beat it for the cabin.

I was standing in the doorway with Mother when the stranger rode up an' touched his funny hat. "My name is George Crook," he said. Mother asked him in. When she started to chunk the fire he said a drink of water was enough but Mother went ahead. In no time she had the frijoles an' the steak warmed up and a pot of coffee, too.

It was so seldom people came I stayed inside the cabin. But he wasn't any fun. The only time he smiled was when I pointed to the jug an' asked him, "How about a nip?" "No thanks, son," he says. Mother's face got red. I was only doing as Dad did whenever people came. I was riding Chappo, had my rifle in my hand an' my six-shooter in my belt, but he never noticed them.

He asked how close the nearest neighbors were. Did the Apaches ever bother? Did the rim-rock trail go clear on through? What about the water? Mother answered all his questions, seemed to be proud he come. He insisted she keep the turkeys, thanked Mother for the meal. He touched his hat again to Mother when he swung up on his mule. We stood in the doorway an' watched him go down the same trail he'd come.

"Who is he, anyway?" I says. "It's General Crook," she said. "If he's a soldier, why don't he dress like one?" Mother couldn't answer. But she said his hat was called a helmet and the funny coat he wore was called a linen duster.

Dad was interested, too, that night when he got in an' Mother told

him General Crook had stopped. She told just what was said. "He's a real
soldier," says Dad, "an' might get something really done if they don't
hobble him in Washington."

"I like Sieber best," I says. An' what Dad said made me feel pretty
good. "If it wasn't for men like Sieber, Crook wouldn't have a chance."

Dad always squalled when he rode in. When he came up the lower

trail, the one that Sieber an' his Apaches used that night, we could hear
him for a quarter. Mother would start to chunk the fire an' smile. The
lines around her mouth would disappear.

I'd be down in the corral waiting, I always helped unsaddle. When he
rode Chappo an' come in early, sometimes he'd let me ride to the cabin
an' speak to Mother. "Well, cowboy, you finally got in," she'd say. It
always made me feel real proud when I rode Chappo alone.

When Dad come off the rim at night an' it was late, Mother an' I would be waiting for his call. Often I could pick it up even sooner than Mother could. I liked to hear Dad's call at night but it made me feel lonesome, too. It sounded a lot like the cry of the loafer wolf that we often heard from the rim.

It was always good to have the cowboys come. Like Dad, they always squalled. Mother could tell their voices, too. "That's Tom," or "That's Bud," she'd say, an' Mother would chunk 'the fire an' start to cook no matter the time of day.

Mother and I were often alone for days when Dad was on the roundup or when he went to Phoenix for supplies. I slept in the big bed with Mother then, she was nice an' warm. When Dad was home, even when he was out on the range, I could play much as I pleased. But when he wasn't coming in at night, everything was different. I couldn't play in my corral because Mother couldn't see me. It was no fun to play all day right in front of the cabin, no matter if Mother did play games with me.

When Dad was away from home we drove the old cow up an' milked with the sun an hour high. The wood an' water was in early, too, an' Mother bolted the cabin door as soon as it was dark. Before we went to bed she always put Dad's rifle on the floor beside her where she could get it quick.

Dad had been gone for several days. Mother was playing a game with me just outside the door, when we heard the cowboy coming up the trail. Never before had I ever seen a cowboy ride so fast. He slid his pony to a stop, looked first at me, then Mother; he seemed afraid to speak. "Go inside, Johnnie," Mother says, "an' close the door." I knew there was something wrong. When I put my ear to the crack of the door I got most of what he said: "Apaches raiding—Old Man Johnson killed—they were heading up this way."

When I busted out of the cabin, Mother let me go with them to the corral. I thought the horse would drop in his tracks when the cowboy unsaddled his pony. Then he slung his gear on Chappo but he didn't want to leave. Mother's face was white an' the lines was in her face. "Go warn the rest of them," she says, "Johnnie an' I'll make out."

When he raked Chappo with his spurs, the horse nearly jumped out from under him. Chappo wasn't used to spurs but he could really run. He was halfway to the rim-rock, going strong, when Mother an' I reached the house.

I helped Mother carry water from the spring; we filled every bucket we had an' carried it inside. Dad had cut a big pile of wood before he left; we carried it all in. Then Mother unrolled the meat tarp and carried in a piece. I could hear the old cow's bell just below the spring. I wanted to drive her up an' milk even if the sun was high but Mother wouldn't let me. Mother did go with me down to my corral; we brought all my horses in.

Mother took the rifle down from the fireplace an' stood it behind the door with the shells Dad kept in the sack. She waited by the door while I kept watch from the window. I don't know how long we waited. I was getting pretty tired when Mother motioned me to her. "They're coming, son," she says.

They were all of a quarter down the trail. Apaches, bucks with rags around their heads, with rifles, too, coming in single file. They were easy to see when they topped the rise, then they disappeared in the brush. The trail didn't open up again where we could see until about two hundred yards of the house. If only Dad was here! I wanted to cry out loud an' I would have, too, if Mother hadn't spoken. "Now, don't get excited when I start to shoot, just keep handing me the shells; we're going to have plenty to do."

Mother had drug up a heavy chair that she used as a rest for the gun; she pointed the rifle over the back of the chair, Mother was on her knees. The door was open a little; but back in the corner where I was with the sack of shells I couldn't see a thing. I figured they ought to be in the open by now where Mother could see the trail. I wanted to get it started, wanted Mother to open up so I could start passing shells.

Then Mother did a strange thing. I saw her uncock the gun; she shoved the rifle away from her an' let it fall to the floor. Then she took me in her arms. Mother was crying, too.

"The Apaches!" I says. "The Apaches—they should be in the open by now!" Mother only held me tighter. At first she couldn't speak. "It's all right, son, it's all right." She finally turned me loose so I could take a look myself—

The Apaches were coming towards the house in single file but Sieber was in the lead. I busted out of the door an' ran to him. I guess Sieber expected me for he handed his rifle to one of the scouts an' gathered me in his arms. The scouts were all around us, but I wasn't even afraid. One of them, almost as big as Sieber was, with a long red scar on his face, poked me in the ribs an' laughed—same as a cowboy would.

When Sieber spoke in Apache all of them scattered out to build their little fires. Mother was glad to see Sieber, too; the lines in her face was gone. She hadn't even chunked the fire or started to cook, she was waiting in the doorway when he carried me up to the house.

BURRO FRENCHY

IX

AN OLD man with powerful shoulders and a barrel chest, he bent forward from the hips as if to ease his tortured back. With both hands he gripped a heavy stick by which he propelled himself along, dragging one broken foot at a time and planting it firmly before he dragged the other foot in place. His movement was not unlike that of an old, hurt bear as he moved up the street.

Aside from an old prospector with a bleached-blue eye, they were cowpunchers, mostly young, who stood in front of the Wellington Saloon on the street in Globe that day. It was thirty years ago. The old man was directly opposite us when the prospector called: "Hey, Burro." At sound of the friendly voice the old man halted, shuffled his broken feet in place and leaning heavily upon his stick he turned his head our way.

Dismissing the punchers at a glance, his face lighted at sight of a friend. To this day I have no idea what he said. When he spoke it was simply a blast. The saloon windows rattled and a cow pony, standing asleep across the street, came alive and looked our way.

His voice was more like a range bull's than anything I know and it carried as much power. When the voice had reached full volume it broke into a screech and, like the range bull's call, the last few agonized notes seemed to tear his insides out.

I was watching the old man drag his battered body up the street when the old prospector said: "That's what the Apaches done to him. He's the only man I ever knowed who took what the Apaches had to give an' lived to tell about it." As we watched the old man moving up the street, stopping occasionally to greet a friend, the old prospector spoke again: "Take a long look, cowdogs, that hombre is all man."

To the old-timers in Arizona he was never Claude Batailleur, one-time corporal in Louis Napoleon's army during the Franco-Prussian War, decorated for bravery; who, later, as a loyal soldier, had fled France after helping put down the French Commune. He was simply "Burro Frenchy."

"Shore, I knowed him," said an old hard-rock miner. "He got in some kind of jackpot in Paris, swum the river and high-tailed it out of

France. Heard him tell it lots of times, but Burro Frenchy's hard to follow, don't speak English good. His name? Never did know his real name, never did ask it, either. It's only been a late thing in Arizona when people ask such questions."

And Burro Frenchy was hard to follow in his talk. It was a mixture of profanity, French, bad Spanish, worse English, with a few words of

Apache thrown in. Being unable to speak French, Spanish or Apache, the first time I went to the old man's house with Joe Sabourin, a mutual friend, I left there slightly dazed. And Burro Frenchy was disappointed, too, at sight of the high-heeled boots, Joe's friend was not a prospector or mining man but one who followed the cows. But Burro Frenchy was hospitable and the old man loved to talk.

He roared for wine at our coming and the very rafters shook. His wife had no sooner served us than he roared again for his "medailes." His wife, lovely in her seventies, and with a soft, sweet voice, brought the Burro's medals. Never boastful, the old man had a fierce pride and he had the look of an old eagle as Joe and I admired them.

He told of his fight with the bear that day and the side walls shook as he spoke. He had been drunker than "seven hunner dollair" when he matched the fight with the bear, drunker than "ze feedlair's beech." And "ze minerail"? It was still in the hills, prospectors nowadays were too damn lazy to hunt! Then he switched to the time he swam the Seine and made his getaway from Paris.

There were other visits to the old man's home and many talks with his friends. He had been in the laundry business in Paris, had owned his own establishment. One year he had been chosen king of the Annual Laundry Festival. The old man was proud of it, too, he had been elected by popular vote.

Coming to America in 1871, he could always turn a dollar; his business instincts were shrewd. He always managed to send something to his wife who ran the laundry business in Paris and to the daughter, born while he was soldiering, whom he had never seen.

As a prospector in search of gold he was known in all the camps in Colorado and New Mexico before he came to Arizona, coming to the mining camp of Globe in 1876. He prospected on Pinto Creek, his tracks were seen on the Gila and through all Apache Land.

With a rich, melodious singing voice, he was a favorite in the dance halls from Trinidad, Colorado, on down to Hovey's on the 'Frisco. As a rough-and-tumble fighter his equal was not known. It was while he was prospecting out of Clifton that he matched the fight with the bear, and old-timers swear it was the first time he was ever knocked off his feet.

After a round of the saloons and dance halls on Chase Creek, the Frenchman had started home. He was on his way to his cabin when a huge bear blocked the trail. He was not only drunker than "seven hunner dollair" that night, he was drunker than "ze feedlair's beech." Thinking it was a man who blocked his way, the Frenchman roared: "Out of my way, hombre," and swung a powerful fist. At which the bear let go with one that not only knocked the Frenchman to the bottom of the gulch, it knocked the Frenchman cold. Burro Frenchy knew very little about

the encounter with the bear except what he was told. Miners going on shift at the time managed to kill the brute.

The Frenchman was different from any white man the Apaches had ever seen. To some he was just a white man, but most of them thought him "touched." Victorio, the chief, thought the Frenchman crazy, and since Victorio's word was law, Burro Frenchy was allowed to come and go at will where any other prospector would have been tortured and killed if captured. Knowing the Apaches would not harm a crazy person or any "blighted one," the Frenchman, more or less an actor, always played the part.

He told of riding into an Apache village, if possible he always stopped in their camps. He never knew what it was all about but he wasn't long in sensing that something was decidedly wrong that day and that he wasn't wanted. Squaws made faces at him behind their hands; Apache children, large and small, pointed sticks and said: "Boom, boom." The Frenchman was thirsty, he had planned to spend the night but he rode right through the Apache camp as if business called him elsewhere. The children who pointed sticks at him and said, "Boom, boom," finally got Frenchy's goat. He was almost through the village, the last Apache boy who pointed a stick and said, "Boom, boom," was big and overgrown. Dismounting, he turned the Indian boy around and, lining his target up, he gave the boy a healthy kick and said, "Boom, boom, yourself."

It was not only the Apaches who thought the Frenchman crazy, there were many whites as well. His manners, the way he talked, and there were always incidents. On one occasion, a charging dog spooked Frenchy's burro who promptly unloaded Frenchy in the dirt. While in a sitting posture, Burro Frenchy shot and killed the dog. The owner, instead of using a gun himself, as was often the case in these parts, had Burro Frenchy arrested and hauled into court.

The Frenchman hired a lawyer; then, ignoring him completely, he said everything he could to convict himself that day. In French, half-English, Spanish and some Apache, Burro Frenchy made his plea. Being excited, the Frenchman not only waved his arms and hands, he used his feet as well. There was nothing for his lawyer to do but wait until he had finished.

"After all, Mr. Batailleur," he said, "you shot in self-defense."

"No fence," said Frenchy, "open country everywhere; no shoot him in ze fence, shoot him in ze . . .!" In one word the Frenchman told how he had hit the dog dead-center as he was going away. It cost the Frenchman plenty; the court not only fined him, his lawyer nicked him, too.

The Frenchman went his merry way through Apache Land, coming and going at will. It was when he allowed a Mexican to talk him into a partnership in a hog ranch on the Gila that the Frenchman's troubles began. Burro Frenchy knew full well that a hog was something an Apache would not tolerate. And he also knew that the Apaches had warred on the Mexicans since the days of Coronado. Always ready to turn a dollar when he could, the Frenchman took a chance.

The partners went to Silver City, New Mexico, and drove in a bunch

of hogs. The ranch was not far from where the little town of Solomonville stands today. The hogs were hardly located when Victorio and his
Apache raiders, who were on the loose, swept down upon the place.

Alone, the Frenchman might have had a chance but his partner lost
his head. The Mexican killed an Apache and died fighting. Burro
Frenchy fled.

It was quite a problem for old Victorio that day. The Frenchman did
not get far. Most of the Apaches wanted Burro Frenchy's blood. Victorio
thought him mad. The old chief finally made a compromise, it was the
best that he could do. The Frenchman was given twenty-four hours by
the sun and headed west, then he was on his own.

Burro Frenchy ran for his life. All through the night he ran, with his
great lungs on fire, sobbing for each breath, resting only a moment, then
on the run again. Catclaw, cholla, desert browse tore the Frenchman's
clothes and flesh. The sun was where it had stood the day before when
the Apaches caught up with him.

Now the Frenchman was stripped stark naked, headed west again and
the torture really began. With rawhide whips and thorny ocotillo stalks
they lashed the Frenchman's naked body; with clubs they knocked the
Frenchman to the earth; with skinning knives squaws hacked him, cut
pieces from his back, rolled him through a cholla thicket the first time
he went down. This was for the squaws and children, the bucks took little
part. Later they would hang the Frenchman head down over a slow fire
while the squaws skinned him alive.

Half-crazed with pain and knowing what was yet to come, the Frenchman kept his head. Knowing his only chance was to convince the Apaches
he was really mad, the Frenchman acted on it. Sitting on his haunches
with head thrown back, he took the coyote's posture, gave its call, starting with its short, sharp bark and ending in its wail. Next he was a rattlesnake crawling on its belly; now the snake was coiled, ready to strike at
anything; he made its singing noise. Now he was a wounded bear, a giant
silver-tip (grizzly), growling all the while he gave the heavy-shouldered
walk the Apaches knew so well. The bear was on his hind feet, uttering
hideous roars; then the big bear charged among them, snapping and popping his teeth as he flailed them with his great paws.

It was too much for the Apaches. Convinced the man was really mad,
that they had harmed a "blighted one," the Apaches fled in terror.

Three days later the Frenchman, stark naked, wounded and bloody from head to foot, crawled into the mining camp at Globe.

The Frenchman never recovered from his ordeal but he lived to prospect again. His voice, which was uncontrollable now, was often the cause of panic when men heard it in the hills. An old freighter said the first time he ever heard the voice it came from a deep side canyon that intensified the noise. His mules went through their collars and his hair stood straight on end. Pulling his rifle from the saddle boot beside the seat, he went to investigate. It was the battered Frenchman with his uncontrollable voice punching his burros along.

Always canny in his dealings, the Frenchman traded, bought and developed claims, usually at a profit. The only sizable wad he ever made while he was in the hills was when he sold his share in a group of claims he held in partnership for twenty thousand dollars.

Burro Frenchy left for Paris. But the homecoming, after all the years, was far from what he had planned. While the laundry business had grown beyond the Frenchman's fondest dreams, the daughter whom he had never seen was horrified at sight of the man who said he was her father.

This was not the handsome corporal with the beautiful singing voice her mother had pictured to her. Her father had been king of the Laundry Festival, elected by popular vote. Nor would the girl be reconciled.

The hurt went deeper in the Frenchman than the Apache knives that day. But before he sailed for America with his wife, he willed the entire laundry establishment to his daughter, also a substantial sum in cash. He never saw her again.

Back in Arizona he took to the hills again. On his burro the Frenchman ranged far and wide in his quest for "ze minerail." His voice was heard on the deserts, it roared and screeched through the hills; intensified in the mountains, it echoed through countless canyons.

Ironically, it wasn't until a brokerage house was started in Globe that the Frenchman made real money. He was too old to prospect then. One of the shrewdest traders on the market, his judgment was uncanny. Somehow the Frenchman always bought when stocks were low and sold when they were highest.

Then, even more quickly than it came, everything was taken away. When he died at eighty-nine there was little property left. But to Arizona

he left a name and a legend: Not Claude Batailleur, corporal of infantry
in Louis Napoleon's army, gallant soldier of France, but "Burro
Frenchy," the crazy prospector, the man who ran the Apache gantlet
and survived.

MAN OF PEACE

X

THE valley lay deep in the heart of Apache Land. The journey had been long. He was fifty-three years old and a grandfather that day in 1876 and he rode a tired pony up the San Carlos trail. As he topped out, the old man reined in his pony and caught his breath sharply at sight of the valley below. For some time he sat his pony, then he spoke aloud:

"This is the place! This is the valley, the valley I've hunted for all my life."

Watching from the valley below, the Apaches missed nothing as the old man rode towards them down the trail. He carried no rope on his saddle, he was not one who followed the cows. He carried a rifle, yet he carried it in the saddle boot and not "at ready" in the crook of his left arm. The old man was not afraid.

That a lone white man would ride among them, unafraid, was something the Apache mind found hard to comprehend. A little pile of rock, the wooden cross that marked a lonely grave was all too common now. Nor was it just an Apache game, the game was played both ways. White men thought less of killing an Apache than they did a coyote.

That the Apaches might resent his coming or do him harm, never entered the old man's head. He had forgotten the rifle he carried in his saddle boot and after waving the Indians a friendly greeting he promptly forgot them, too. There was something far more important on Grandpa Harer's mind that day. After twenty-five years he had found it, the valley he had hunted so long.

When he and the tired pony drank from the springs that bubbled from the thicket of locusts and blackjack oaks, the water was clear and cool as the mountain air that filled his lungs. Grass stirrup-high covered the broad flats. The stream from the bubbling springs that flowed through the valley was crystal-clear, its banks lined with tules.

As his eye swept the valley it was just as he had pictured it, almost as far back as he could remember. He would build the cabin here, here by the bubbling springs. The pens and corrals would be shaded by the locusts and blackjack oaks. As he looked, the waving grass that covered the broad flats became fields of rippling corn. And he could see the hogs, fat hogs; for Grandpa Harer was from Arkansas.

Man in his hunt for happiness often seeks strange things. Unlike many men, Grandpa Harer always knew what he wanted. When he hooked the mules to the loaded wagon that April morning in 1851 and left Arkansas with his wife and baby girl on the trek West, it was not in search of the rainbow's end. The gold in California held no interest. Nor did he want land that could be had for the taking, or grass for the cattle. Grandpa Harer wanted a hog ranch. It was more than a hog ranch he wanted, though; not just a place to raise hogs. Somehow there was always a valley, he could picture the sort of place in his mind.

During the journey across the plains with the wagon train, there was no trouble with the Indians, but often they were hungry. Grandpa told of killing small birds with his rifle and how Grandma would make soup for Mary Elizabeth, the baby. A cow was yoked to the wagon when one of the work mules died.

In Tulare County, California, Grandpa raised wheat and prospered. Yet he was not satisfied. Finally he reached Oregon. There were beautiful valleys in Oregon but never the one that he sought. Back in California again, the search went on and on.

When he first came to Arizona in the early '70's, Grandpa worked for a time at Hayden's Mill on the south bank of the Salt. He was farming in Salt River Valley, raising sorghum and hogs, when he first met Captain Hancock.

The captain was stationed at Fort McDowell. Aside from the bacon and hams he cured, the captain liked Grandpa, and Grandpa often spoke to him of the valley he hunted. The valley had become an obsession, he could picture it in detail. And unlike many other men, the captain was interested; he saw things in pictures, too.

The captain had been on two weeks' scout with a troop of cavalry on the Tonto. The night he got back to the fort he hunted Grandpa up when he had dismissed his troop. And the captain was excited. "I think it's the place," he said.

The troop had ridden through Reno Pass, crossed the Tonto and rode up Salome Creek. There was a big butte on the right. They had ridden up Salome Creek to where the San Carlos trail had crossed; they had followed the trail from there. "I saw it just as we topped out," the captain said, "an' it hit me in the face. But the valley is full of Apaches. I had a troop of cavalry with me, one man would not be safe." Yet in spite of the warning from his friend, the next morning, long before the morning star had set, Grandpa was on his way.

He built the log cabin by the bubbling springs. There was a rock fireplace chinked with adobe. He made the roof of tules. He cleared the land and ditched the fields, cut logs and built the pens and corrals, put in a sizable orchard.

Of medium height, with powerful shoulders and narrow hips, at fifty-three he was as active and quick as a cat. Yet how he ever got a

loaded wagon into the valley alone is still a mystery to his descendants.

The valley had been a favorite camping ground of the Apaches as far back as their old men could remember. In no other valley did the beyotas (acorns) grow as sweet. It was not far from where they gathered the saguaro fruit and had their mescal pits.

One thing they could not understand: the old man sang as he worked. A hymn that was a favorite of his the Apaches knew by heart:

> "There's a land that is fairer than day
> And by faith we can see it afar,
> For the Father waits over the way
> To prepare us a dwelling place there
> In the sweet by and by—"

That he had taken their valley—was an intruder—never entered Grandpa's head. There was plenty for all, he said. The fact that it had been Apache hunting ground for over three hundred years and that the Apache might have another point of view never occurred to him.

And the Apaches did have another point of view as far as white men were concerned. While their broad valleys along the rivers were being taken by men with hairy faces who farmed and followed the plow, the cowmen with herds of longhorn cattle were pushing deeper into the hills. The Apache fought in his own way; it was his hunting ground. The cowman, who had come to stay, fought him in turn with always the lurking fear in his heart that his family might be murdered at the lonely ranch house while he was out on the range.

It was into this setting that Grandpa Harer came; Grandpa, the man of peace, into the fight of "dog eat dog." And the Apaches, whatever their feelings may have been when he first came to the valley, came to call him Salmann (friend).

If an Apache wanted to hunt and had no ammunition, Grandpa gave him some. If the Indian had no rifle, Grandpa loaned him his gun. When Old Nosey picked up a pair of horseshoes, put them in his shirt and rode off, Grandpa followed pronto. He simply told Nosey to give him the horseshoes and he gave the Apache a lecture on how wrong it was to steal.

This was a new approach as far as the Apache was concerned; he couldn't understand. He had stolen and been caught. Any other white man he had known would either have shot him off his horse or jerked him from his pony and whipped him with his pistol. Old Nosey pondered deeply, he couldn't understand. But next day he hunted Grandpa up and stated simply, "No more steal from Salmann."

Aside from a big Newfoundland dog that had followed him from California, and the Apaches who camped with him, Grandpa stayed alone in the valley that year. When he left on occasional trips to Salt River for supplies and a visit with the family, the Apaches were left in charge. There was one trip, however, he hadn't counted on.

The big Newfoundland dog didn't share his master's feelings when it came to the Apaches. He never did like their smell. One evening the big dog thought an Apache was too close to Grandpa and growled. Grandpa spoke sharply to the dog and thought no more about it. But next morning when Grandpa hit the floor at daybreak, there was no big dog to greet him. The dog's feelings had been hurt and he had pulled out for home in the night.

Knowing the family would be worried if the dog came in alone, Grandpa caught a horse and followed. He had got as far as Sugar Loaf

when he met his friend the captain. Captain Hancock had seen the big dog pass the fort alone just as it broke light. Thirty minutes later he was on his way to hunt his friend with a small detail of cavalry.

Grandpa had been in the valley a year when he went to Salt River and brought in a hundred hogs, driving them in afoot. Pork had always been held in abomination by the tribe; a hog was something an Apache would not tolerate. Yet the Apaches made no protest. Aside from calling him "Ole Hog Capitan" occasionally, they ignored the hogs completely. As soon as Grandpa had located the hogs he brought his family in.

Of his neighbors, who were cowmen, some said the old man was balmy, others called him "touched." Why would a man raise hogs and farm, raise feed, kill hogs, render lard, cure hams and bacon, then haul it sixty miles in a wagon to Globe or eighty miles to Phoenix? Now, with a steer—the critter simply lived on grass an' walked afoot to market.

He actually made friends with the Indians; some said he even went so far as to loan an Apache his gun! Whenever there was an Indian scare or a settler murdered, the cowmen said that "old Sweet Bye an' Bye had went an' spoiled the dirty varmits."

In the '80's, during the Pleasant Valley War, maybe as high as thirty men were killed. One night some of the Graham faction might be camped at Grandpa's place, the next night it might be the Tewksburys. Folks wondered how Grandpa stayed neutral through it all. The fact that he treated everyone alike and refused to speak evil of any man, refused to speak at all unless the word was good, might have meant something to them. While the cowmen stole each other's cows and fought, Grandpa raised hogs and prospered.

When Jake Loafer crawled in one night with a bullet wound and a broken leg, it was Grandpa who probed for the bullet and set Jake's leg, while Grandma nursed him through. Jake had only been gone three days till he was back again. This time he rode a horse. It seems Jake had managed to cut his foot half off while he was chopping wood.

To turn a hungry person from the door, red or white, was a sin as far as both Grandpa and Grandma were concerned. She cooked for all who came. And no trail was ever too rough or the night too dark for Grandma to ride a horse alone if some neighbor needed nursing or some woman was expectin'.

And while Grandpa never wore a ring in his nose, Grandma—a

person in her own right—had a way of snubbing him up short when she thought the occasion warranted. Though a man of deep convictions, he was never one to preach. There was only one occasion when Grandpa ever tried it; it might have been the audience. The cabin was full that day—there were children and grandchildren present—when Grandpa began to speak upon the evil of strong drink. He was warming to his subject, too.

"David," said Grandma in her quiet voice, "don't preach, it's unbecoming of you. I've seen you so drunk that you fell off your horse." Grandpa was flustered, yet he always spoke the truth. "That's right, I was drunk an' I fell off the horse. I was a young man then, but I know better now."

Grandpa didn't like to kill anything that wasn't necessary; he never cared to hunt. But one son-in-law, Florence Packard, was a mighty hunter of panthers and bear. Wearing moccasins, he followed his dogs afoot. When a rancher offered him a horse, Florence Packard refused, saying that he wanted nothing with him on a hunt that he couldn't pack on his back. Farming held no interest for Florence. He pursued the varmits relentlessly, often hunting them at night. Yet somehow he managed to find the time to father twelve fine children, and Grandpa built a schoolhouse.

Aside from Florence's brood there were other grandchildren, too, and several waifs an' strays that Grandpa and Grandma raised. The first teacher was a woman, and while Grandpa was a man of peace, not all his grandchildren were. The school was hardly under way until the children ran her off.

Grandpa brought in a man next term. The new teacher was one-eyed, with a broken nose and crooked smile. He was tall, with sloping shoulders and hands that hung almost to his knees. And Grandpa was innocent about the whole affair. He had never seen a prize fighter in his life. The children were innocent, too. Some of them were big, gangling boys in their teens; this intruder was only another teacher to them and without preliminaries they planned to put him on his way. The affair was short and sweet; when it was over, teacher's knuckles were skinned up some but he still wore his crooked smile. There was not a boy who ganged him who wasn't on the floor.

They still speak of that little school in the valley and how well-mannered the children were. There was never a school on the Tonto that had such discipline.

Aside from his feeling for the Apaches, Grandpa Harer liked snakes, too. He said there was no harm in most of them. He went so far as to pull the fangs on a rattlesnake and kept it as a pet. Josie, sixteen and pretty, was a favorite granddaughter of his. One day when she was teasing him he said, "Let me alone, now, Josie, or I'll put the snake on you." Josie thought the snake was harmless, for Grandpa had pulled its fangs. In the scuffle that followed, the snake bit Josie on the arm and Josie nearly died. Yet she protested in her delirium that it wasn't Grandpa's fault. Even Grandpa didn't know there were other fangs that grew. He felt terrible about the whole affair and promptly dispatched his pet, the rattlesnake, and would have no more of them.

The Apaches still camped in the valley, coming and going at will. It was July and August when the Indians came in droves. Sometimes as many as two hundred would come streaming off the hill. Bucks always riding singly, squaws riding loaded ponies with children up behind; Indians afoot and squaws with loads upon their backs a white man could hardly lift. Squaws and children laughing and chattering, waving to their friends. They had come not only for the saguaro fruit and to gather the beyotas, but to visit Grandpa and his family.

Apaches from the San Carlos Agency, they traded calico, blankets, sugar and white flour that had been issued at the post for corn and dried fruits that came from Grandpa's orchard. And always they brought presents.

There was Grandpa with his warm smile, shaking a buck by the hand, and Grandma bustling about. Children, red and white, chasing each other, playing games and visiting quietly since they had not seen each other in months.

In his thirty years in the valley, aside from the pair of horseshoes Nosey took, there was only one other thing that an Apache ever stole. It was a favorite mare of Grandpa's, stolen by a renegade Apache from the reservation, who killed the mare and cut steaks from her flank.

The neighbors, who were white men, didn't score as well. Any fat hog that wandered off Grandpa's range was apt to disappear. Grandpa said the hog became confused, lost all sense of direction and couldn't find his way home. Yet he knew where they went.

When renegade Apaches were raiding in the hills, Grandpa would sometimes send the family to the Fort but he never went himself. Neighbors were murdered by the Apaches, their stock was driven off and killed. Grandpa and his family never were molested.

The cowmen finally came to respect him. Unlike his friends the Apaches, they never quite came to understand the simple man of peace who raised hogs instead of cattle and who lived by the Golden Rule.

When Grandpa finally took the long trail at eighty-three, the long trail that all men, red and white, must ride alone, it was the Apaches who mourned his passing. For four days, each morning as the sun rose and each evening as it set, their wailing filled the valley:

"Salmann, Salmann, Salmann—"

TWO BITS

XI

"SO YOU'VE joined the Army!" She spat the words into his face. "None of you Crofts was ever worth two bits; you'll never have two bits." She stormed into the house and Private Croft let her go. They had often quarreled—he had always called her back—but she had never spoken like this before. He watched her until the door closed. Then he mounted and spurred his big horse into the night.

Inside the house she sobbed hysterically as she heard the big horse splash across the creek. She was at the door as he clattered up the steep bank but Private Croft did not look back.

Private Croft never rode that way again and she married a man named Martin while Croft was serving the first year of his enlistment in the United States Cavalry at Fort Whipple, Arizona. A civilian scout brought the news to the post. "A big affair it was—two fiddlers an' two barrels of whiskey. Martin had done it up big, the bride was purty as a picture. They made a fine-lookin' pair."

Private Croft heard it all from his narrow bunk, and whatever his feelings may have been, outwardly he gave no sign.

That a rookie's girl had married another man—well, it was too good

a thing to let pass. The troopers attempted coarse jokes at his expense. They didn't get very far. One night on the picket line he went berserk an' tried to kill Private Burns when Burns, in his quiet way, said he'd rather milk a dozen cows and have a woman waiting for him than be a captain in the army. It was a lucky thing for all concerned that Sergeant Rafferty heard the fuss. Burns was unconscious and the rookie still had him by the throat when the sergeant pulled him off.

Private Croft might have made a good soldier. Sergeant Rafferty thought so, at least. A good shot with both rifle and pistol, he had a way with a horse. Never excited or jumpy, he was a good man to have in a fight. With his knowledge of Apaches and the country, Croft was always at his best when his troop was in the field.

And the fierce pride the rookie had in everything he did was something the sergeant liked. After his affair with Private Burns, the troopers let him alone; as Burns said, it wasn't good to stir up a wildcat, six feet tall, that weighed a hundred an' ninety pounds. The troopers might have taken him in, but he seemed to prefer his own company. The rookie made no friends.

Sergeant Rafferty thought it was a passing thing—just give him a little time. It was no more natural for a kid of twenty-one to keep to himself than for a colt to not want to play. But as the months slipped by and the kid lived more within himself, it bothered the grizzled old sergeant. One night when the two were alone on scout and the Arizona moon was riding high, the sergeant spoke to him.

"I did me first hitch because of a girl; she married another man. I took it hard, meself, at first, but it's ten kids she's had since then. Can ye fancy me with a brood like that on a farm in Illinois? I tell ye, yer lucky, son. Soldierin' is the life, me boy, ye have the makin's too."

The sergeant meant all right and the private heard him through, but when he spoke his eyes were cold. "You go to hell," he said.

Croft's troop was the only one at the fort when news of the raid came in. Someone had to get through to Camp Verde. When the C.O. called for volunteers, it was Private Croft who went.

It was dark when he left Fort Whipple and climbed the trail that wound up the mountainside. There was nothing to fear until daybreak; night time was sacred to their ancestral dead, the Apaches seldom struck until dawn. The sky was showing gray in the east when his big horse splashed across Lynx Creek and climbed the other side.

From Lynx Creek the trail climbed to a plateau with hardly any cover for almost thirty miles. Then it climbed again to descend a steep, bare mountain slope into Verde Valley. From the mountains, the Apaches could spot a rider for almost twenty miles. When Croft saw Apache smoke signals on three sides he knew that he'd been seen.

He was halfway across the big plateau when the Apaches made their move. From a distance the dust their ponies' feet kicked up looked like little puffs of smoke. He had eased the big horse along, now he moved him from a long gallop into a dead run.

He heard the slugs whine past him, watched them kick up puffs of dust. An Apache seldom cleaned a gun; it was hard for him to get that front sight down; they had always been poor shots. The horse he rode was a Morgan—they have always had big hearts—and he was running smoothly, moving with even strides.

But life and death have usually hung on little things. The big horse was beginning to pull away when a stray slug found his heart. Croft felt the Morgan quiver and for an instant he seemed to hang almost in mid-air. Then the big bay horse went down.

It was a few days later that a detachment found Croft's body on the divide. He had made his way to a little knoll and made his stand with a pistol; his rifle had been broken when the big horse fell. It was hard to tell whether he had been alive or not when the Apaches closed in. The pistol was empty, every chamber had been fired. The C.O. found it half buried in the sand and he looked at it a long time.

He carried it with him to Camp Verde. That night over a glass of bourbon he spoke of Private Croft. "I wouldn't have ordered any man out; Private Croft was the only man who volunteered, and knowing Apaches as he did, Croft knew what it meant. But the request he made before he left is the thing that puzzles me. 'I'll go for two bits,' he said. He made me give him a quarter. I wonder what could have been in his mind."

BLAZE OF GLORY
XII

HE HAD the sharp, hard eye and the pallor of the gambler. There was no mistaking his trade. A small man and dapper, with slender fingers and sensitive hands. Plucking a miner or cowhand was simply routine with him. Always affable and polite, in a game with range men he looked effeminate. It was not misunderstood. He had killed his man on the street in Globe and the affair had caused no little comment in the little mining camp. The gambler had not taken the odds as was expected of his kind. The deceased had fired two shots and missed before the gambler went into action. And he had been promptly acquitted.

As a boy soldier during the War Between the States, he had turned his first card on a blanket. Some say he was wounded then. His right leg had been shattered below the knee and he was forced to walk with a cane. After the Civil War he had drifted West with the tide. Felix Knox was the name when he came to Arizona.

Gambler, saloon man and killer, there were two things that set him apart. In any game he didn't ask for the best of it, and the dance-hall girls did not exist as far as he was concerned. Knox was a family man. There were two children; he was married to a Mexican girl and he was deeply in love with his wife.

She was watching his hands as he held the reins; they were soft and sensitive. But the back of his hands was brown, and the pallor, the deadly pallor of his face, was gone. Felix's nose was sunburned.

As a Mexican girl, petite and pretty, it was only natural that she should make comparisons. She had been proud in Silver City when men touched their hats, patted the muchachos on the cheek and called her man by name. The grizzled old foreman had taken a little one on each knee at the ranch where they stayed last night. One cowboy was handsome; she had dropped her eyes at his glance. He had helped Felix hook the mules to the buckboard less than an hour ago and he had deferred to Felix. Her man was a gambler and not one who followed the cows.

Always she had doctored the poor leg when Felix came in from his work. There had been potions from deep in Mexico; each time her hopes

had been high, yet nothing seemed to help. And the muchachos—no matter the hurt in his leg or how late he got in, he always walked to their bed and smiled down as the little ones slept. Some nights the sky had been gray in the east, yet she always waited for him.

She would tell at a glance if the luck had been good. There was one night she would never forget. He had made her sit on the bed and close her eyes, promise not to open them until he gave the word. She knew they were rings he placed on her fingers; it wasn't until she opened her eyes she saw they were diamonds and how big and blue were the stones. And she had felt sorry for Felix that day when he came and took them away. Her man was a gambler and Felix had needed money.

The muchachos still slept in the seat between them, in spite of the jolting rig. The mules were trotting steadily as Felix flicked the reins. One more night on the road and the little ones would sleep in their own bed and she would wait again for Felix in the little house in Globe.

The first shaft of morning sunlight was touching a distant peak. Felix was watching it, too, but why would he pull the mules to a walk? It was then she saw the Apache smoke signal rising high on a distant ridge. Now Felix had stopped the mules. The road was narrow here. He had turned the team and started back to the ranch when up ahead the guns went off and they heard the whine of the leaden slugs.

Now he lashed the team into a dead run. For a time they held their own. Then the pace began to tell. As the Apaches gained steadily upon them, the gambler studied his ground. Just ahead the valley narrowed up; there was no cover but they could not by-pass him here. He moved so swiftly she scarcely knew what had happened. She was holding the reins, then she realized he was gone.

He had given each one of the children a pat on the head, hers was a peck on the cheek. He hadn't spoken a word, but he'd smiled down at her as he went over the seat with his rifle and the ammunition belt. As he dropped to the ground behind the rig, she had not seen the shattered leg give way. But the sights of the rifle were both in place; he had protected the gun when he fell.

She knew the shooting was faster now and the slugs no longer whined. The mules had slowed to a trot. She was trying to quiet the little ones when the shooting suddenly stopped.

She was in sight of the ranch when the cowboys passed her, going into the fight, their horses on the dead run. The grizzled old foreman was in the lead, holding his carbine high. They had yelled and waved their guns at sight of her. She knew they were too late.

Hours later, she sat dry-eyed and heard the old foreman speak. "There was no cover. He had been hit many times by the slugs. Empty shells lay all about him. The heavy ammunition belt was empty. He had fired every shell in the belt.

"The Apaches had done a strange thing, the body was not mutilated. They had folded his hands across his breast as if he were asleep. They had covered his face with his own silk handkerchief, weighting each corner down with a little white stone as respect to one who was brave."

She heard it all for the sake of the little ones; sometime they would know and be proud. It did not soften the hurt. Never again would she wait at night until her man came home from work.

BROTHER TOM

XIII

THERE are some things a man always remembers, never forgets until he dies. I won't forget the look in Sam's face that day on Pinto Creek when we buried his brother Tom. What the Apaches had done to him is still unspeakable, after more than fifty years.

As friends we had gone with Sam on the hunt for his brother. Tom had been long overdue. We had identified the body. It made me sick all over. We only tried to make it easier on the boy, tried to spare his feelings some. But Sam wanted to be certain in his own mind that it was really Tom.

As he looked, his body stiffened; he didn't speak a word. When he turned away he was dry-eyed, yet there wasn't a man amongst us who missed that look in his face.

He stood alone as we wrapped the remains in a blanket. It was a shallow grave. There was no preaching or service of any kind. None of us knew what to say. Sam helped carry rocks and boulders that we piled in a heap on the grave. He helped Old Al set the little cross Al made from palo verde. We rode to the brow of the hill and waited while he stood alone by the little pile of rocks and boulders and the little wooden cross.

Back in town Sam bought a round of drinks after we'd unsaddled at the corral and turned the horses in. "Thank you, gentlemen," he said. "I appreciate what you've done today."

It sounded stiff and formal; we might have been total strangers instead of Sam's best friends. Then he gave us a little formal bow, the kind that only a well-raised little boy has been taught to give. He walked into the street alone.

The brothers had come to Arizona from the South, one couldn't miss their talk. Soft-spoken, well-mannered and quiet, they were always together whenever Tom hit town. In their early twenties and tall, with

black hair and eyes, they could have passed as twins. Together on the
street or at the bar, they were a pair one couldn't miss.

Tom was the prospector, spent most of his time in the hills. Sam
worked steady in town. As partners, it was Sam who furnished the grubstake. He had a way with figures, kept several sets of books.

I know Tom often tried to get Sam out in the hills with him, if only

for a trip. Sam wanted no part of it. One night when the three of us were
at the bar, Sam said: "That's your end of the deal, Tom, you like it;
mine is to furnish the grubstake, keep things going here. Before I'd
punch a burro through the hills an' live like a coyote, I'd sooner get a tin
bill an' pick with the chickens—at least I'd be in town."

Yet it was less than a week from the day we buried his brother on
Pinto Creek that Sam got an outfit together and went into the hills alone.

We seldom saw him after that. He was out for weeks at a time. He'd
come in just long enough for his grubstake that he earned by keeping
books. In town he not only turned the clock around, he worked both night
and day. Never did stay long. Several men offered to grubstake him, as

Sam didn't throw off any. He punched his burros far and wide; wouldn't take a pardner, though, always went it alone.

During the time that Sam was in the hills—an' it run better than a year—there were several small strikes made. Two of the boys struck it pretty big on ground Sam had already covered. Sam never found a thing.

The only money he ever made was when he traded claims; it was one his brother had located. The claim Sam traded for went into the group that later became the Old Dominion Mine. Sam got five thousand for that one and left Globe, left for good this time.

I was interested in mining those days, myself—always had a few claims. Fact is, that's where my nickname came from. Lots of old-timers didn't know that Charlie was my name. I put up so many location notices an' markers they called me "Monument Clark." One group I owned looked pretty good. I had high hopes at the time. Nothing ever came of it, but I was called into New York.

It was noon. People in flocks an' droves were pouring into the street. I was down on lower Broadway, just happened to be looking into the little cemetery in the yard by Old Trinity Church. Even in death they were crowded. It had been fifteen years since the Apaches had killed the boy we buried on Pinto Creek; at least, he had plenty of room.

Someone had stopped beside me. I didn't turn until I heard the voice: "Monument Clark, I believe, sir, who comes from Arizona!"

Sam hadn't changed much, aside from his tailored clothes. He was glad to see me, too. He owned a little brokerage house. Sam called it a "bucket shop." I went home with him that night for dinner, met his wife and two fine boys. They owned a nice place on Staten Island and I enjoyed the ferry ride.

Sam and I talked late that night. He asked of everyone. I tried to give him all the news. Folks come an' go in a mining camp, an' Globe wasn't just a camp of tents an' shacks, the place had really grown.

I saw a lot of Sam in the week that I was there. We went to the theatre twice; when I didn't go home with him an' spend the night, he ate with me in town. Sam was happy, too, in his wife and two fine boys. New York suited him. Yet in our talk, and no matter what the subject, he'd come back to Arizona. He didn't mention his brother Tom; we skirted Pinto Creek.

The day I left we had lunch together at a little place downtown, had English mutton chops and ale. I was feeling fine, the mining deal looked pretty good an' I was heading home.

"You know, it's funny, Sam," I says, "in all the time that you were out, you never found a thing. It was there an' on the surface, too. There was that ground you covered—" That was what touched him off. He had that look in his face again, the look he'd had that day on Pinto Creek when he saw what the Apaches had done, how they had tortured his brother.

"Prospecting!" he says—his laugh wasn't pleasant to hear. "Prospecting! Hell, I wasn't prospecting; I was killing Apaches. I got twenty-nine for brother Tom."

BLOOD BROTHERS
XIV

THE CHIEF of the fighting Chiricahuas sat beside his wickiup. Wrapped to his waist in a bright Mexican blanket, he was drowsing in the sun. There was snow on distant peaks. The air was clear and cold but in the shelter of the wickiup the sun was warm and good. It was the latter part of January, the year was 1861.

The dozen wickiups in the little group were exactly like his own. Nor was there any distinction in his dress, aside from a heavy army shirt. He wore the clout and long Apache moccasins. The snows of more than fifty winters had flecked his hair with grey. It was bound with the red flannel band that most Apaches wore. It was in other ways besides his dress that Cochise stood apart.

A giant for an Apache, the chief stood six-feet-two. His belly was as hard and flat as any warrior's in his band. Cat-like in his movements, he walked with easy grace. In intellect the old chief's mind matched the stature of his body. There was another thing that set the chief apart in any group, red or white—he always spoke the truth. The old chief scorned a liar.

The fighting Chiricahuas had always been at war with the Mexicans. As a young warrior, his first fight had been against them. There had been countless fights and raids against Mexicans before he rose to be the chief. The first Americans from the North, the mountain men and trappers, had been another race.

There were Apaches who would kill them all; the intruders were all alike. Too many Americans were coming in. Cochise had given it much thought. It was better to get along. At times some of his younger warriors were hard to hold. But he had always kept the peace.

As Cochise drowsed beside his wickiup, there was a stir in the little camp. A squaw delivering wood at the stage station had seen a company of soldiers pass. The soldiers had gone into camp about a mile below the station.

There was nothing to be excited about. The officer might be one of his friends. He would make the soldiers a call. Yes, his brother might go with him as well as his two nephews. As the horses were being led in by the squaws, the old chief's eye fell on his little son. He would take the boy and his mother, too.

Second Lieutenant George N. Bascom of the Seventh Infantry wel-comed Cochise. The chief had walked into his hands. Once Cochise and his party were inside Lieutenant Bascom's tent, soldiers surrounded it. Through an interpreter the lieutenant stated his mission.

Four months before, in October, Apaches had raided Ward's ranch on the Sonoita, had stolen Ward's adopted son and ran off stock. Ward had trailed the raiders far enough to be convinced they were Chiricahuas, a part of Cochise's band. Riding to Fort Buchanan, he had asked the troops for help. Bascom did not explain the several months' delay in starting on his mission, but he demanded of Cochise that he return the stolen boy and stock.

Cochise replied that neither he nor any of his band held the Ward boy or the stock and knew nothing about the affair. It was later proven that Cochise spoke the truth. A band of Pinal Apaches had been the guilty ones. Cochise stated, further, that he would investigate, find out what band was guilty and if possible he would have the boy and the stock returned.

It was here that the young lieutenant, only two years out of West Point, made the first of his frightful mistakes. He accused Cochise of lying. The chief was his prisoner now; he would hold him and his people as hostages until the Ward boy was returned. The words were hardly spoken until Cochise escaped.

Drawing a knife from his breech-clout, the old chief slashed the tent. He had leaped through the guard that surrounded the tent before the soldiers collected their wits. Taking advantage of each bit of cover, he avoided the volleys the addled soldiers sent crashing after him; running like a startled antelope, he made his escape to the hills.

It was not long until a column of smoke, like a thin grey thread, rose high into the sky. The smoke signal was repeated from distant ranges as the word was passed along. When darkness fell, the signal fires were

burning on distant peaks. The chief of the fighting Chiricahuas was calling his warriors in.

A wagon train was captured and burned. Two men were taken prisoner; two others were burned alive. The eastbound stage from Tucson was ambushed and attacked not over a mile from the station. The driver was badly wounded, one of the lead mules killed. As the Apaches fired from behind brush and rocks, passengers cut the dead mule from the traces, and Buckley, superintendent of the line, mounted the driver's seat. He had reached the stage station and safety when a wheel mule dropped dead in the harness. Three men who were watering the stock at the station were caught in an ambuscade; two of the men were wounded, the third the Apaches killed.

In the meantime, Lieutenant Bascom had moved his troops to the station and dispatched a courier in the night to Fort Buchanan for medical aid. Buckley dispatched a courier to William Oury in Tucson with a request that the message be relayed to troops at Fort Breckenridge. Both messages were delivered.

It was about this time that Cochise, with three prisoners he had taken, rode to within earshot of the station. One was Wallace, a stage driver, who spoke the Apache tongue. Always friendly to the Apaches, Wallace had been captured by subterfuge; not knowing of the trouble in Bascom's camp, when the Apaches had called to him, he had walked unarmed into their hands.

Through Wallace as interpreter, Cochise demanded the return of his relatives, offering to release the three white men in return. Lieutenant Bascom refused; he said there would be no exchange of prisoners until the Ward boy was returned. Again Cochise replied that neither he nor any of his band had any knowledge of the Ward boy's whereabouts or of the stolen stock.

Baffled, the old chief rode away but he was back again next day.

This time Wallace's hands were tied, the other end of the lariat was tied to Cochise's saddle. Once more, through Wallace, Cochise asked that his relatives be released; he would set the white men free. Wallace said he had already suffered much at the hands of the Apaches, he knew it meant death by torture if Lieutenant Bascom refused.

At this point, Sergeant Bernard, who later rose through the ranks to Brigadier General, added his entreaties to those of the prisoner Wallace;

and he was so insistent, Bascom placed him under arrest. Once more the lieutenant stated that there would be no exchange of prisoners until the Ward boy was returned.

When Bascom turned and walked away, Cochise dragged Wallace to death behind his running horse. Later the other two white men were put to a cruel death.

With the arrival of troops from Fort Buchanan and Fort Breckenridge, Cochise and his Chiricahuas scattered like mountain quail. An Apache village was found and burned but no Apache was seen. Cochise's scouts ranged far and wide, any move on the part of the soldiers was quickly reported to him. Smoke signals went up on distant peaks. At night the signal fires burned. It was at this time that a young Chiricahua scout rode in to see the chief.

Six Apaches were hanging in an oak tree not far from the soldiers' camp. He had driven away the carrion birds and identified the bodies. Three were Coyoteros who had been captured in a running fight when they had encountered the soldiers from Fort Buchanan hurrying to Bascom's relief. The other three were Chiricahuas; two were Cochise' nephews, the other was his brother.

Now the fire so stupidly started was fanned to a red-hot flame. It was to burn through twelve long years of bloodshed and ruin. Scattering his warriors in small bands, Cochise directed the fight.

In the summer of 1861 word reached Arizona of the War Between the States. Federal troops were ordered withdrawn. Believing that they

were responsible, the Apaches redoubled their efforts. It was only in Tucson or at some mine or ranch, where the whites gathered and fought to the death, that the Apaches were held in check. Ranches and mines were abandoned. Arizona was desolated.

At the end of that long, bloody struggle, troops were sent into the Territory to punish the warring hostiles. The stage lines were opened again. Once more the whites were coming in numbers and they were coming to stay.

Now the year was 1867. A tall, red-headed rider had watched his Apache friend build the smoke signal. At first, a small handful of dry grass and twigs, then more dry wood and when it was flaming fiercely, green stuff was thrown on the blaze. And he had watched the thin column of smoke rise higher and higher into the blue sky. Then, with a wet saddle blanket over the fire, the Apache had made a series of dots and dashes in smoke, unintelligible to the white man but telling the Chiricahuas that the lone horseman riding toward their camp was on a mission of peace.

For some time the tall red-head and his Apache friend squatted on their heels, their eyes intent upon the dark and brooding mountain that lay beyond the great valley. As they watched, the answer came. High on the timbered slope a slender column of smoke was rising, blue-grey against the ridge.

"Smoke say 'come,' " said the Apache. As he spoke, he mounted his pony and turned back. When the tall rider headed his horse into the great valley he was alone, alone with his thoughts.

The tall red-headed rider was Tom Jeffords. As a prospector, trader and scout, he spoke the Apache language. He carried arrow wounds in his body, shot from ambush when he was driving stage. Only recently he had resigned as Superintendent of United States Mail from Fort Bowie to Tucson because the troops could not protect his carriers. He had helped bury too many Apache victims, killed by torture, not to understand their ways.

The tall rider knew the odds he faced. He gambled on one thing: men who had known the old chief before the fireworks were touched off had always respected him. Though he had been fighting these many years, he had been friendly to the whites until the series of frightful blunders had started the long and bloody war.

As he jogged slowly across the great valley, a lake of still water appeared. As he looked, the mirage became a river that called back other years when he rode a River Packet on the Mississippi instead of a jogging horse. He had come to know the old river; he'd been proud as a Captain, too. Yet something had always called him farther and farther west. When the river vanished before his eyes and the dust devils again appeared, the brooding mountain that lay ahead called up other moun-

tains, the mountains of his youth. But the mountains of his boyhood in
New York State had been soft and friendly things. That was long years
ago. He was thirty-five years old.

What would the old chief say? What would he do? It wouldn't be
much longer, anyway, until he knew the answer.

And the Apaches missed nothing of his coming, as the lone horseman,
mile after mile, jogged slowly towards their camp. At first he was but a
moving dot in the great valley. When the broad valley narrowed, smoke
signals went up as he passed. The lone rider not only carried a six-shooter
in his belt, he carried his rifle "at ready" in the crook of his left arm.

As he rode into the Apache camp, the hostiles were all about him and
there was no friendly face. Speaking in Apache, he asked for the wickiup
of the chief. And when the tall rider swung down from his horse he was
the first white man in many years to face the old war chief, and live.

Handing his rifle and sidearms to a squaw, Tom Jeffords addressed
the chief: "I have come for a talk," he said. "I may stay a couple of
days. I expect my arms to be returned to me when I am ready to leave."

Cochise, who had never taken his eyes from the white man's face,
disdained to make a reply. Nor could the tall red-head guess the answer
as he looked into the old chief's face; only his dark eyes seemed alive,
the face was immobile as granite.

How long the two men faced each other Tom Jeffords did not know.
When Cochise finally turned away and seated himself in the shade
beside his wickiup, Jeffords followed and sat beside him.

For some time he sat in silence, as was the Apache custom, then
Jeffords spoke again: "My mission is not official. I speak only for myself.
I have heard that you like straight talk. I have a living to make. What I
want is a peace, a peace between you and your tribe and myself, where
I can go about my business and not be molested by any of your warriors."

When he had finished speaking, the chief made no reply. The shadow
from the wickiup was slowly growing longer. Even after the old chief
began to speak, Jeffords had no idea what the outcome might be.

But on the second day a squaw brought his saddled horse. Cochise
returned his arms. Jeffords was given an armed escort to see him safely
across the big valley. His cool and quiet courage had won the old chief's
heart. The chief had known brave men before; this white man's nerves
were ice. The two men had talked at length; the white man's talk was

straight. It was the beginning of a friendship that lasted through the years.

Later, through an Apache ceremony, the two men became blood brothers. And while Jeffords, as a scout, was often called to guide troops against his friend, Cochise always understood. Their friendship was never broken.

There were five more years of bloodshed, the killings went on apace and through it all Tom Jeffords rode unharmed.

When General O. O. Howard was sent to Arizona by President Grant in 1872, to make peace if possible with Cochise and his fighting Chiricahuas, there was only one man who could make the contact. General Howard found Jeffords in New Mexico acting as scout for a cavalry column.

When General Howard asked Jeffords if he could take him to Cochise' camp, Jeffords looked long and searchingly into the General's eyes before he spoke:

"Will you go there with me, General, without soldiers?"

"Yes, if necessary," the General replied.

"Then I will take you to him."

Jeffords promised General Howard he would meet Cochise at the end of seven days, and at the General's request he allowed Captain Slayden, the General's aide, to accompany them. After securing two Apache guides, whom Jeffords knew were close to the heart of old Cochise, the party left Fort Bayard.

Sending up smoke signals from time to time that the mission was a peaceful one, and traveling steadily westward, at the end of the seventh day General Howard met Cochise. The old chief, after being introduced to General Howard, looked at his friend.

"How long have you known these men?"

"About a month," replied Jeffords.

"Will they do as they say they will?"

"I don't know," replied Jeffords, "but I think they will."

It took five days for Cochise to call in his sub-chiefs who were out raiding at the time. In all, it took eleven days to make the peace. Cochise was given a reservation in his own country that was acceptable. His only stipulation was that Tom Jeffords act as agent. Jeffords wanted no part of it.

It not only meant considerable financial loss to him, he knew the headaches involved. But he, too, was tired of the senseless killing. At Cochise' and General Howard's insistence, he accepted on certain terms. There was to be no meddling or politics, his word would be absolute. No soldier, civilian or official of any kind was to come on the reservation without Tom Jefford's consent. He was to report directly to the Department of the Interior instead of the Indian Bureau. General Howard, who had been given wide powers by President Grant, approved Jefford's request.

The bond of an Indian agent was usually ten thousand dollars. Jefford's bond was fifty thousand. Honest, efficient, fearless, Tom Jefford's word was law. With his friend Cochise beside him, peace came to the Chiricahuas. Stolen horses and cattle held by the Chiricahuas were returned to their rightful owners.

On several different occasions, hostile bands of Apaches on the warpath contacted the fighting Chiricahuas, tried to lead them out. Cochise had given his word to keep the peace; he kept it until he died.

Jefford's name with Cochise was Chickasaw (brother). They were together much and talked of many things. Jeffords said Cochise's religion was "truth and loyalty."

"Chickasaw," said the chief one day, "a man should never lie."

"No," replied Jeffords, "he should not, but a great many do."

"That is true," said Cochise, "but they need not do it; if a man asks you or I a question we do not wish to answer, we could simply say: 'I don't want to talk about that.' "

The old chief was not a simple man, his nature was complex. He loved and hated much, got drunk and beat his wives. Trained in an age-old school of savagery, yet he gave much thought to what might happen after death.

The two friends had been together two short years when Cochise became ill. Jeffords had provided medical aid but the old chief had been failing steadily. He knew it was the end. Jeffords had been with his friend for several days when he was called into the Agency. As they said good-bye, both Jeffords and Cochise knew the end was not far off, nor did they attempt to hide it.

"Chickasaw," said the old chief, "do you think you will ever see me alive again?"

"I don't think so," said Jeffords; "I think that by tomorrow night you will be dead."

"I think so, too," Cochise replied. "Tomorrow morning about ten o'clock. But do you think we will ever meet again?"

At this his friend was taken back. "I don't know," he said. "What do you think about it?"

"I have given it much thought," the old chief said. "I think we will meet again."

"Where?" asked his friend and blood brother.

"Somewhere up there, I think." And the old chief of the fighting Chiricahuas pointed to the sky.

The next morning Cochise had his warriors carry him up the slope to watch his last sunrise. He died that day at ten o'clock, as he told his friend. He was buried that night in his stronghold; all night long his warriors ran their horses up and down the canyon until all trace of his grave was gone.

Now a mountain in Arizona and a great County where he ranged bear the name of the famous chief. But to this day no white man knows exactly where he sleeps. Tom Jeffords, blood brother, who survived his friend by forty years, carried the secret to his grave.

AGENT CLUM

XV

GERONIMO, cruelest and most cunning of all the Apache renegades, surrendered to the military on several different occasions, but he was captured only once. He was taken prisoner by John P. Clum, civilian Agent at San Carlos, and Clay Beauford, Captain of the Apache Police. This was the same Geronimo, with less than forty followers, who surrendered to General Miles nine years later. At the time of the surrender, General Miles had five thousand regular troops and three hundred Apache scouts in the field.

Clum was a farm boy of Dutch ancestry from New York State who had come to Santa Fe, New Mexico, in 1871, to work in the newly organized meteorological service which later became the National Weather Bureau.

In those days, different churches sponsored the various tribes of Indians, and the Apaches were the special province of the Dutch Reformed Church. So the call came to Rutgers University for someone to accept the dubious job of Apache Agent. Clum had attended Rutgers for a year before he came West, and some of his friends, knowing he was in New Mexico, recommended him for the job. When Clum accepted, his salary was sixteen hundred dollars per year and travel expenses.

In spite of his youth—he was not yet twenty-three—Clum had many qualifications. He had intelligence, he was honest and he had a sense of justice which, when applied to the Apaches, was an unusual thing in those days. And the young Agent had the knack of picking men to work with him. Sweeney, his chief clerk, had served in the cavalry for fifteen years; Clay Beauford, whom Clum appointed captain of his Apache Police, knew Indians and soldiering.

Hated and feared by the citizens of the Territory, the Apaches had been on the reservation only a year and a half and in that period there had been a succession of agents, both civilian and military. Only recently,

Lieutenant Almy, United States Army, had been killed at the agency; teamsters had been murdered. There was no distinction between good and bad Apaches, renegades had been allowed to go unpunished. Apaches indulged in tulapai, their native drink. Clum's predecessor, having seen Lieutenant Almy killed, departed for Tucson pronto, the only white habitation within two hundred miles.

The young agent took stock; as far as he could observe there had been no coordinated policy in regard to the Apaches. He had made the trip to Washington to inform himself of all that had gone on before he accepted the post and he learned from the records that thirty-eight million dollars had been spent in the years from 1862 to 1871 to either exterminate or roundup the Apaches. Yet Clum found their birthrate was slightly on the increase. As he dug deeper into the reports, he realized his government, presumably protecting the Apaches through its Department of the Interior, was at the same time endeavoring to exterminate them through the Department of War.

As far as the Apaches were concerned, John Clum believed that any combination of military and civilian authority was doomed to failure; if the Apaches were treated fairly, there would be no need for any soldiers. Clum clashed with the military at San Carlos at every turn. He may have had his faults but the young Agent was genuinely interested in one thing, the welfare of the Indians.

Both civilians and soldiers in Arizona, for the most part, shared one conviction: "The only good Indian was a dead Indian." Clum believed that there were good and bad Indians; that the Apache was, at least, human and he acted accordingly.

One of Agent Clum's first acts was to disarm the Apaches. If an Apache wanted to go hunting, he was issued a rifle and a pass; at the expiration of his pass, the Apache turned in his rifle. He wanted the Apaches, as far as possible, to learn to administer their own affairs. He set up a court with himself as chief justice where the Apaches acted as both judge and jurors. He appointed four Apache police.

This pleased the Apaches as it was the first time in their dealings with the whites on the reservation that they had been treated other than as prisoners of war. The civilian population in Arizona literally howled. And the military hooted: there had been civilian agents before, given a little time they would put this young upstart in his place!

Clum's first test with his Apache police came when he was informed that some Apaches were making tulapai in a canyon a few miles from the Agency. Now tulapai, when taken in large quantities, has always been a potent drink. To this day on the Reservation it is still a problem. The young Agent went with his police on the raid that night; they brought in the culprits who were tried and sentenced before an Apache jury by Apache judges.

News has always traveled fast in open country; Apaches began to filter into the Agency. In a few months Clum had a thousand Indians under his official wing. However, when the government transferred fourteen hundred Rio Verde Apaches to San Carlos, Agent Clum's major test began. The Verdes were embittered by this forced move from a Reservation the government had solemnly deeded them, where they had dug their ditches and planted their fields. They split in factions and fought among themselves coming over the trail. And Agent Clum had not been notified until the transfer was being effected.

At their first powwow, a few days later, Clum told the Verdes they must turn in their guns. The powwow broke up at once, the Verdes left en masse. Returning to their camp, they mounted their horses, waved their guns defiantly and moved to a new camp a few miles up the river.

Ration day on the Reservation was Saturday; ration tickets were issued to every man, woman and child, even to nursing babes. The Indians were counted. Clum stepped it up a day, completely ignoring the Rio Verdes. Rations are something an Apache loves to this day; all Apaches love to eat. That evening the Rio Verdes sent Clum seventy-five rifles as a token of surrender. On Saturday, to the astonishment of the Verdes, Clum and Sweeney rode alone into the Verde camp, where Clum issued ration tickets and gave orders for the count.

In later meetings he explained to them in detail his policy. He had the chiefs appoint several police from among the tribe whom he approved. He also appointed Verdes to sit on the Apache court.

Hardly was this headache over when Clum was ordered by Washington to Camp Apache, sixty miles north of San Carlos, to relieve the agent there. That agent, too, had been having his troubles with the military. Fort Apache, the Army Post, and Camp Apache, the Agency, were located on opposite sides of White River about a mile apart. The affair had climaxed when Captain Ogilby sent a detachment of troops across the river and took forcible possession of the Agency.

In following out this order from Washington, Clum was blocked in every attempt by the military. "Come over and see us, Clum," said the captain. "We'll always be glad to see you socially and we'll fight you officially as long as you wish."

Clum ordered a count of the Coyoteros at the Agency; Captain Ogilby ordered them to the Fort to be counted. It was the captain who finally backed down, however, when he found Agent Clum could not be bluffed or intimidated. Later, without military escort, Clum and George Stevens, an Indian trader whose wife was a Coyotero, with forty of Clum's Apache police, brought in fifteen bands of Coyoteros to the San Carlos Agency.

On May 3rd, 1876, Clum was ordered to proceed to the Chiricahua Reservation, take over that Agency in Apache Pass and, if practicable, remove the Chiricahua Apaches to San Carlos. Once more our government not only broke faith with the Apaches, it broke its sacred word.

The Chiricahuas, most warlike of all the Apaches, under their great war-chief, Cochise, had spread terror in southern Arizona from 1861 to 1872. With General O. O. Howard acting as intermediary, Cochise made peace; was given a reservation of his own, with Thomas Jeffords as agent. Cochise and Jeffords were not only friends, through a ceremony they had become blood-brothers. It was only on the consideration that Jeffords become agent that Cochise consented to go on the reservation. Cochise kept the peace as long as he lived.

The sons of Cochise, Tahzay and Nachee, had pledged their father on his death to keep the peace. It was these two sons of the old warrior under Clum who, in spite of the government's broken promise, led their band of three hundred and twenty-five Apaches to San Carlos. Some of the fighting Chiricahuas, under Geronimo, Ju, Nolgee and other sub-chiefs, fled to the Sierra Madre Mountains in Sonora, Mexico.

In this transfer, Clum again tangled with the military. General Kautz, of the Department of Arizona, refused to cooperate until ordered to do so by the War Department. But it should be said to General Kautz' credit that he offered Clum an escort of cavalry to Apache Pass. This escort Clum refused, taking his Apache scouts instead.

Clum now had over four thousand Apaches at his agency and since the military had been removed from San Carlos he thought most of his troubles were over. The Apaches were farming in a small way; those who worked were paid at the rate of fifty cents a day. Clum issued script. He bought hay and grain from the Apaches; as a matter of fact, everything they produced. He bought livestock for them, both sheep and cows. It was Clum who built the Agency at San Carlos without outside contract labor. While many of the tribes, moved to the agency, were none too friendly, at least they were getting along. The young agent liked his job. He was proud of the Apaches and proud of what he had done.

It was while young Clum was reflecting that the following telegram came:

> Washington, D. C.
> March 20, 1877

Agent Clum, San Carlos, Arizona
If practicable, take your Indian police and arrest renegade Indians at Ojo Caliente, New Mexico. Seize stolen horses in their possession; restore property to rightful owners. Remove renegades to San Carlos and hold them in confinement for murder and robbery. Call on military for aid, if needed.

> (Signed) Smith, Commissioner

Clum acted at once. Sixty Apache police had been trained by Clay Beauford and under his command were serving as a roving police force for the Governor of the Territory of Arizona. Clum sent a courier to the Governor requesting the use of these scouts, which was promptly granted. He also notified Beauford to meet him on an appointed date at Silver City, New Mexico. He wired General Hatch, in New Mexico, of his assignment, requesting him to place troops for the protection of citizens in southwestern New Mexico should his assignment go amiss.

And the following day, Clum and forty Apache police, with two wagonloads of supplies, set out afoot on the four hundred mile journey to Ojo Caliente. At Fort Bayard he received a reply from General Hatch stating that he had not only made disposition of his troops for the protection of the citizens, he was sending Major Wade with three troops of United States Cavalry who would meet Clum at Ojo Caliente.

Although there had been no mention of his name, Sweeney, whom Clum had sent into Ojo Caliente to scout the place, brought Clum word that Geronimo was the leader of the hostile band. While Geronimo was little known at this time, Clum had met the renegade once before, when he was removing the Chiricahuas from Apache Pass to the San Carlos Reservation. And Agent Jeffords had told Clum of the band of southern Chiricahuas raiding back and forth from Mexico into Arizona and New Mexico, that Geronimo would be hard to handle. The renegade did, however, have a talk with Clum; he said his band was scattered and asked two days to round them up and bring them in. But Geronimo, as usual, broke his word, rounded up his band and fled to the mountains of Sonora, Mexico.

Having secured some horses in Silver City, New Mexico, Clum took twenty-two of his Apache police and rode into Ojo Caliente on the evening of April 20th. There he received a telegram from Major Wade that he and his three troops of cavalry would be a day late. Clum reflected; he knew if he waited a day alone with his twenty-two scouts, it would not be healthy for his contingent. Clum knew, too, that if he made the attempt to capture the renegade alone and failed, the responsibility was his own.

Clum made his decision: he sent a courier to Captain Beauford, ordering him to move the rest of the police into the agency during the night, come as quietly as possible, hide his men in the big commissary

building that was empty. And the next morning at daybreak he sent word
to Geronimo to come in.

Canny as Geronimo was, he had been tricked; he thought Clum had
only his twenty-two Apache police with him. He came early that morning with his entire band which numbered about one hundred. With six

of his Apache police, Clum stood on the agency porch; Beauford and the
other sixteen were arranged in a semi-circle. Geronimo and six sub-chiefs
stood directly in front of Clum, defiant and arrogant.

When Clum told Geronimo the purpose of his mission, the renegade
replied in no uncertain terms. He had no intention of going to San Carlos;
he added, further, that if Clum was not careful, he and his Apache police
would not return to San Carlos, either.

The showdown had come sooner than Clum expected and for the
first time in his life, young John P. Clum wished for the military. Unlike

the early "Western," there was no cloud of dust, no soldiers. Clum gave the prearranged signal: nonchalantly, he touched the rim of his broad-brimmed hat with his left hand and the commissary door swung open; his reserves poured out in single file and on the dead run, each man with his rifle "at ready," to form a great half-circle.

Clum had not taken his eyes from Geronimo; he saw the old rene-gade's thumb creep slowly towards the hammer of his rifle. Clum gave the second signal: as his right hand touched the butt of his six-shooter, Beauford and the twenty-two Apache police covered Geronimo and his sub-chiefs with their guns. As Clum watched, the old renegade's right hand moved back, away from the hammer. Yet when ordered to tell his followers to lay their guns on the ground, Geronimo did not speak. Then, at a slight nod from Clum, Beauford moved in, covering Geronimo di-rectly with his rifle.

Handing his six-shooter and belt to one of his Apache police, young John P. Clum walked down from the porch, and Geronimo made no move as Clum relieved him of his gun. It was the first and only time the rene-gade was ever captured. Disarming the rest of Geronimo's band was simply routine.

When Major Wade and his three troops of cavalry arrived next day, Geronimo and six sub-chiefs, wearing leg irons, were under guard in a stout corral while the rest of the renegade's band sat and visited with Clum's police. In small groups they were scattered all about the agency. This was part of Clum's belief in the Apaches; he knew that an Apache squaw, like her white sister, prefers the path of peace to that of war. It had worked with the Verdes, the Coyoteros and the Chiricahuas; given a little time, his missionaries would prevail upon the renegades. Clum an-ticipated no trouble.

While still at Ojo Caliente, Clum received two telegrams: the first, advising him to take Victorio, chief of the Warm Springs Apaches, and his band of three hundred and forty-three, to the San Carlos Reservation along with the renegade Chiricahuas. The second telegram was to the effect that other hostile Chiricahuas were raiding out of Mexico.

Clum replied to both requests. He dispatched Beauford with seventy-five Apache police on the trail of the hostiles. With a detail of twelve soldiers, under Lt. Hugo, he brought Geronimo and his band of rene-gades, Victorio and his band, a total of four hundred and forty-three in all, to San Carlos; marching them from Ojo Caliente, New Mexico, a distance of four hundred miles.

Back at San Carlos young Agent Clum was rewarded, yet not in the way one would imagine. He had completed every assignment given him. He had consolidated five agencies into one, at a saving of approximately one hundred thousand dollars per year to his government. The Apaches under his jurisdiction had increased from eight hundred to five thousand, while Clum still drew his original salary. Although the Commissioner in Washington had pledged the young agent the fullest support of the Indian Bureau in any interference by the military, on his return to San Carlos Clum found a company of soldiers camped at the agency.

John P. Clum had learned much about Apaches in three years at the San Carlos Reservation but he was still a very young man as far as the game of politics was concerned. A business friend in Tucson gave him a lead: "What are you trying to do, ruin my business?" he asked. "If you take the military contracts away from us, there would be nothing left worth staying for; most of our profit comes from feeding soldiers and army mules!" The welfare of the Apaches was incidental when political pressure was applied in Washington.

Clum had planned to make the Apaches his life's work. He forced a showdown when he sent the following telegram:

> Tucson, Arizona,
> June 9, 1877

To the Commissioner of Indian Affairs
Washington, D. C.

> If your department will increase my salary sufficiently and equip two more companies of Indian police for me, I will volunteer to take care of all Apaches in Arizona—and the troops can be removed.

> (Signed) John P. Clum
> U. S. Indian Agent

The Commissioner in Washington gave copies of the wire to the press. The Brass Hats had a field day, verbally cowhiding the "young civilian upstart who offered to accomplish, with two hundred Apache police, what two thousand soldiers had failed to achieve in seventeen years."

After Clum's resignation there was again a succession of agents, military and civilian, both good and bad; and each agent had a policy of his own or no plan, whatsoever. Through such confusion one wonders why more Apaches didn't leave the reservation and return to the warpath.

Clum had planned that Al Sieber and Clay Beauford should head the Apache Police, both men probably knew Apaches as well as any men of their time. In light of the nine tragic years that followed young Clum's resignation, it is interesting to speculate what might have been accomplished if the plan he believed in had been put to work, since Clum was only interested in one thing—the welfare of the Apaches.

THE WHITE MAN'S WAY
XVI

THE lieutenant had exceeded his authority, but the small garrison at Old Camp Grant was ready in case of treachery. The lieutenant watched with mixed emotions as the Apaches neared the Post.

Eskiminzin, the chief, and Old Santos, his father-in-law, were in the lead. There were sixty warriors in the band. A few carried rifles, the rest were armed with lances, bows and arrows. There were no horses. They came afoot and in rags. There were no blankets and in many instances there were no moccasins; many walked with bloody feet. There were young men who carried litters on their shoulders, they carried the sick and those too weak to walk. Old squaws carried wide-eyed, half-starved Apache children and their pitifully few belongings on their backs. There were young squaws with sunken breasts who walked slowly beneath the weight of cradle-boards that cradled hungry babies.

There were one hundred and fifty in the ragged, half-starved band of Aravaipa Apaches who moved slowly towards the Post that March morning in 1871. The commanding officer, First Lieutenant Royal S. Whitman, was not a West Pointer. A veteran of the Civil War, he had risen from the ranks to Lieutenant Colonel of Volunteers, and in 1867 had been commissioned Lieutenant in the 3rd Cavalry, United States Army, and assigned to Old Camp Grant, Arizona, in 1870.

When Eskiminzin had come personally to ask for peace and permission for his starving people to once more plant their little fields in the fertile valley of the Aravaipa, a few miles from the post, the lieutenant granted his request; he believed Eskiminzin was sincere.

The lieutenant told the chief that while he had no authority to treat with him, he would consult his superiors as to the final disposition of the Apaches. In the meantime, he not only allowed the Aravaipas to set up their wickiups on the fields that had been their homeland for generations, the lieutenant issued food and blankets and promised Eskiminzin and

his band the protection of his troops. He encouraged them in their work
and the little fields, idle over five long years, once more took form.

Other Aravaipas began to filter in and it was not long until Lieutenant Whitman had five hundred Apaches under his official wing. Aravaipa
children learned to laugh again. Lieutenant Whitman wrote in his
official report to Colonel J. G. C. Lee, his commanding officer, at Tucson:

"These Aravaipa Apaches, especially their chief, Eskiminzin, have
won me completely. The men, although poorly clothed and ignorant,
refuse to lie or steal; the women work like slaves to clothe their babies
and themselves and, though untaught, they hold their virtue above price.
They need help to show them the way to higher civilization, and I will
give them this help as long as they are permitted to stay with me."

But all was not peaceful in Arizona and the Apache problem was far
from settled. Cochise and his fighting Chiricahuas still raided in southern
Arizona. Small bands of hostile Tontos, Coyoteros and Pinals ranged the
hills. A delegation of Tucson citizens appealed to General Stoneman,
Commander of the Department of Arizona: "The five hundred Aravaipas under Eskiminzin were a menace!" They bitterly protested the protection given to the Indians by Lieutenant Whitman and his troops. There
could be no distinction between a peaceful and a hostile Apache. The only
good Indians were dead Indians. When a small band of Pinals killed a
white man on a raid near San Xavier, the powder was touched off.

Under the leadership of W. S. Oury and Jesus M. Elias, six Americans, forty-eight Mexicans and ninety-two Papago Indians set out to exterminate Eskiminzin and his band. The Adjutant-General of the Territory furnished the arms and ammunition.

To avoid suspicion the party left the Old Pueblo in little groups for the rendezvous at Pantano Wash. Captain Penn, commanding officer at Fort McDowell, having wind of the affair, sent a courier to warn Lieutenant Whitman. But the raiders had planned well; mounted guards held up the courier and turned him back to Fort McDowell. Captain Penn then sent Sergeant King to warn Lieutenant Whitman, but the sergeant was too late.

At dawn on the morning of April 30, 1871, Oury's party struck the sleeping village and the bloody work began. At first no shots were fired, Papagoes with war clubs slipped silently into wickiups and brained everyone who slept. The screams of helpless women and children soon roused the entire camp. With rifles and revolvers, whites and Mexicans now played their bloody part. Women who begged for mercy were mercilessly shot down. Children who fled screaming were pursued and brained by Papagoes or shot down as they ran. And there was the sickening smell of burning flesh when the wickiups were fired.

Oury and his party had planned well; while many escaped to the hills, the bodies of one hundred and eighteen Aravaipas lay strewn about the camp. While only eight were men, the bloody, mangled bodies of one hundred and ten women and children were proof that the work had been well done. There were prisoners, too, twenty-seven Apache children were taken to be sold into slavery.

When Sergeant King rode his lathered horse into the post with Captain Penn's warning, Lieutenant Whitman immediately dispatched couriers to warn Eskiminzin. The lieutenant ordered his troops out; they were ready to march in defense of the Aravaipas when the courier returned. The Aravaipa camp was a shambles, there was not a living thing in sight.

Lieutenant Whitman led the burial detail. As he offered a prayer for the dead Aravaipas who had been his friends, hard-bitten troopers wept openly, unashamed. As the grief-stricken survivors watched from the hills, they realized that Lieutenant Whitman and his troops had had no part in the ghastly affair. One after another and in little groups they came to mourn their dead. One of the last to come in was the chief, Eskiminzin. In his arms he carried a little girl, the only member of his entire family who survived the massacre.

The lieutenant took Eskiminzin and the survivors to the post. After a few days they again set up their wickiups on their little fields. But it was less than a month until a party of soldiers from Fort Apache, hunting deer, rode unexpectedly upon the camp. Believing the Apaches to be hostiles, the soldiers fired. Once more the Aravaipas fled to the hills. But Eskiminzin and Santos, his old father-in-law, came first to Lieutenant Whitman to disavow the peace.

"The peace you have promised to the Aravaipas," said Eskiminzin, "has been broken, not once but twice and each time by the Americans. We now go back to the mountains to avenge our dead." Nor could Lieutenant Whitman reply.

News of the massacre caused a storm of indignation and protest in the East. When President Grant threatened to place Arizona under martial law unless the guilty were punished, they were indicted, tried and promptly acquitted. To most citizens of the Territory, the only good Indian in Arizona was a dead Indian.

Of the twenty-seven children taken as prisoners, six were later returned. The fate of those sold as slaves into Mexico was never known.

Later, W. S. Oury, a prominent citizen in the Territory and leader of the band who made the attack, wrote of the ghastly affair: "The Papagoes attacked them in their wickiups with clubs and guns. Not a single man of our command was hurt to mar the full measure of our triumph and at eight o'clock on the bright morning of April 30, 1871, our tired troops were resting and breakfasting on the San Pedro a few miles above the Post in the full satisfaction of a work well done."

When Eskiminzin disavowed the peace he had made with Lieutenant Whitman and fled to the mountains with his band, he killed a white man,

a man who had been his friend. Later, when asked why he had killed a man who had befriended him, the chief replied: "To teach my people that there must be no friendship between them and white men. Anyone can kill an enemy but it takes a strong man to kill a friend."

Yet Eskiminzin was never a warrior like Cochise of the fighting Chiricahuas or Victorio, chief of the Warm Springs band, who, with many of his band, died fighting in the basin of the Tres Castillos in Old Mexico. He did not hate the whites as Old Nana, whose hatred burned within him like a flame and who, when he was in his seventies, made his greatest raid. Nor was he like the renegade Geronimo who asked for peace and always broke his word.

The Aravaipas were the least warlike of all the Apache bands and it was Eskiminzin, in spite of his great personal tragedy, who always counseled peace. Cochise fought for over ten long, bloody years to avenge the death of his brother and two nephews who were hung by soldiers; and Cochise is said to have made good his boast to kill ten whites for every warrior lost. The only known white man Eskiminzin ever killed was when he fled Camp Grant.

Eskiminzin was a realist. But two trails lay ahead. The murder of his family did not blind him at the councils of his people. He saw the two trails plainly. He chose the one that led to peace in spite of personal feelings, for the other trail that led to war could only mean the extermination of his people. Within a few months he came in alone. Word had reached him in the hills of a man who came from Washington.

This man, Vincent Colyer, was a member of President Grant's Indian Commission. Through an interpreter he and Eskiminzin talked. Colyer had read the story of the Camp Grant massacre and at his request Eskiminzin, in halting sentences, told again the tragic story; and he told of "Lieutenant Whitman of the good heart," how he and his soldiers had mourned and buried the Aravaipa dead. When Eskiminzin asked that he and his people be allowed to return and live with Lieutenant Whitman and his soldiers, Colyer, the Quaker, was deeply touched. He would do all in his power for the Aravaipas and he would send word to Eskiminzin in the hills whenever the word was good.

But as the months slipped by and no word came, Eskiminzin came again to Old Camp Grant. Colyer was gone but Eskiminzin talked with General O. O. Howard. General Howard was a personal emissary of

President Grant who had given him wide powers. General Howard knew the tragic story; he told Eskiminzin to bring all his Aravaipas in, they would be issued food and blankets and until a suitable place for a reservation could be found, he would establish a temporary reservation for the chief and his people near Camp Grant.

Eskiminzin and his people lived at Camp Grant until the San Carlos Reservation was established in 1872. Seven thousand square miles was set aside for Apaches who wanted to live in peace. By midsummer in 1873, bands of Coyoteros, Pinals, Warm Springs, Chiricahuas and Tontos had come to join Eskiminzin and his Aravaipas who planted their little fields along the San Carlos river. Eskiminzin and his peaceful Aravaipas were happy. But their happiness was destined to be short-lived.

Many of the half-wild bands roamed the high country. Government agents came and went; aside from issuing rations, they made no attempt to know their wards. The white man ruled by fear alone; soldiers were insulting and arrogant. It was resented by the Apaches; undercurrents grew. No distinction was made between good and bad Apaches, who brewed their tulapai in the open and went on glorious drunks. It was after one affair that four drunken Chiricahuas killed two teamsters. When the drunken Indians came back and boasted of the affair, all the Chiricahuas, fearing the innocent would be punished with the guilty, left the reservation and headed south for Mexico.

It was Eskiminzin who called the council of the chiefs. Soon the white soldiers would come, he said; they would not ask who killed the team-sters, everyone would suffer. And that night, when the moon was full, all the remaining Apache men, women and children fled the reservation.

When news of the killing reached Fort Apache, all troops were ordered out. A stupid man in a position of high authority usually runs true to form. No attempt was made to search out the killers and punish the guilty ones. Orders were issued to pursue the fleeing Indians and *to take no prisoners*. The order to take no prisoners was rescinded, however, when Captain Hamilton, in disobedience of the order, refused to shoot a starving band of Coyoteros and allowed them to surrender.

Eskiminzin and his ragged band were the last to come in. In March, 1874, three months after they had fled the reservation, he led the Ara-vaipas to San Carlos and surrendered to the agent. There were no charges against the Aravaipas. Aside from running away, they had com-mitted no crime. But misfortune and injustice walked once more at Eski-minzin's side. Major Randall, the Commanding Officer at Fort Apache, ordered Eskiminzin and his six sub-chiefs placed in irons. With leg irons riveted to their ankles, the prisoners were taken to New Camp Grant where for nearly six months they worked in chains under military guard.

Old Camp Grant had been abandoned, New Camp Grant lay further east. It was here that John P. Clum, enroute to take over his duties as Agent at San Carlos, saw his first Apache Indians. He was particularly attracted to one prisoner who, in spite of his chains and the leg irons riveted to his ankles, moved with quiet dignity. The prisoner was none other than Eskiminzin, the Aravaipa chief.

"What are the charges?" asked the agent. "Major Randall doesn't like him," the officer replied.

Through an interpreter Clum was allowed to interview the prisoner. It was through Clum's efforts that Eskiminzin was later released; it was the beginning of a friendship that lasted through the years.

When the young agent arrived at San Carlos he knew nothing about Apaches and he had need of friends. None was closer to him than the Aravaipa chief who not only counseled his own people but the other bands as well. Eskiminzin had another family now and, like the young agent, he believed that since the Apaches were to live in peace they must become self-supporting by farming and stock raising. For three years no Indian worked harder than the Aravaipa chief.

When Clum resigned in 1877, Eskiminzin had a long talk with his friend. Now that his friend, the agent, was leaving the reservation, he was leaving, too. He would take up land on the San Pedro and follow the white man's way. For if trouble came to the reservation after his friend had gone he feared he would be blamed.

When Eskiminzin and his family moved to the San Pedro and took up their farm, the land was valueless. They cleared the fields of brush

and stumps, dug irrigation ditches. How well they succeeded is better told by Lieutenant Britton Davis who stopped enroute to Tucson, ten years later and had a meal with Eskiminzin and his family.

"The little colony of six or eight families might well be mistaken for a colony of prosperous Mexican families. They had adobe houses, fields under barbed-wire fences, modern (for those days) farming implements, good teams and cows. They dressed as the Mexicans in Arizona dressed— cotton shirts and trousers for field work, a suit of 'store clothes' for important affairs: dances, Sundays, feast days, etc.

"In Eskiminzin's house a greater surprise was in store for me. His wife and children in their Sunday best of bright calicoes were introduced to me. The dinner table was set in the living room with a clean, white cover; plates, cups, knives, forks and spoons at each place. Substantial chairs for the grown-up four of us. Mrs. Eskiminzin and the younger children served the meal, a very well cooked and appetizing one as I remember it. For the occasion Eskiminzin had on a store suit of coat, vest and trousers; adding to it a near-gold watch with a heavy silver chain of which he was very proud and by which he had learned to tell the time after a fashion.

"Dinner over, a young man appeared with a light buggy and a remarkably good team of horses, well kept and eager to go. Eskiminzin proved himself a skillful driver.

"At Tucson he took me to see several merchants with whom he did business. These men told me that Eskiminzin ran accounts in Tucson totaling several thousand dollars, and that his credit was good for four or five thousand in the principal store there should he desire it for himself or his people."

But once more misfortune befell the Aravaipa chief. White settlers wanted his land. Captain Pierce, hearing of the affair, sent Lieutenant Watson to warn the chief who was taken to San Carlos. This warning, no doubt, saved Eskiminzin's life. Shortly after he had left his ranch an armed mob came from Tucson and drove his family off.

Back on the Reservation, Eskiminzin was given a piece of land. The chief started all over again. Once more he cleared the land and ditched the fields—but misfortune struck again. The Apache Kid, most feared of all the outlaws of the late '80's and early '90's, had married one of Eskiminzin's daughters. It was said Kid's outlaw trail often led to Eskiminzin's door. There was no proof nor was the old chief given a hearing, he was arrested and sent in exile to Alabama and held as a prisoner of war. But let Eskiminzin tell his story as it stands today in the files of the War Department at Washington—

"When I took up a ranch on the San Pedro I had three horses and twenty-five head of cattle. I was on the San Pedro ten years; then I had seventeen horses, thirty-eight cattle, a large yellow wagon for which I paid one hundred and fifty dollars; four sets of harness for which I paid forty dollars and another wagon which cost ninety dollars but which I had given to some relatives. I also had many tools.

"For about three years I drew rations from the Agent. After that I did not draw any more till I was sent to the Agency by Lieutenant Watson (seven years later). I bought all my family clothing and supplies with the money I made.

"About four years ago (1888) Lieutenant Watson came to my ranch and gave me a paper from Captain Pierce, the agent, and he told me that citizens would kill me if I did not; that there were about one hundred and fifty citizens coming with pistols. They came next day after I left my ranch and they shot at my women, putting bullets through their skirts and drove them off.

"They took five hundred and thirteen sacks of corn, wheat and barley, destroyed five hundred and twenty-three pumpkins and took away thirty-eight head of cattle. I took my horses, wagons and harness with me to San Carlos. I am not sure that the citizens took the thirty-eight head of cattle at this time. I only know that when I came back to my ranch next time they were gone.

"Captain Pierce said that I could select a farm on the Reservation. So I went with Lieutenant Watson and selected a piece of land on the Gila just above the sub-agency. Lieutenant Watson surveyed it for me. I made a ditch for irrigating and had water flowing in it and had nearly finished fencing the farm when I was arrested.

"When I was arrested I had twenty-one horses and six head of cattle and these have since increased to thirty-eight horses and sixty-eight cattle. Since I have been away one wife and some of my children have looked after the farm for me."

It was his old friend, John P. Clum, who, after twenty years, was to intercede for him again. Clum found the old chief working at Mount Vernon Barracks, Alabama, as a prisoner of war. Unlike their first meeting, twenty years before, the chief was not in chains. A model prisoner, he was acting as head gardener. Eskiminzin, armed with a pitchfork, was building a compost heap. The two men had not seen each other for fifteen years. At first Eskiminzin, busy at his work, did not recognize his friend. But as recognition grew, he stared incredulously. Clum was the first to speak: "Hello, Skimy"; he spoke casually as if their meetings were an every-day affair. The next instant John P. Clum was wrapped in the old chief's bony arms.

Nor was the old Apache chief bitter, his white friend found it hard to understand. He had suffered the massacre of his family, imprisonment at hard labor, the loss of his lands and, finally, exile. From the day he came into Old Camp Grant and asked for peace, misfortune and misunderstanding had walked at Eskiminzin's side. No Apache who had

tried to follow the white man's way had suffered more than he. Yet as
Eskiminzin and his old friend talked, Clum found no rancor in his heart.

It was through Clum's efforts that Eskiminzin was released and sent
back to his people at San Carlos. But the old chief was not destined to enjoy his freedom with his family and his people, his happiness was short-
lived. A few weeks after his return, Old Eskiminzin died.

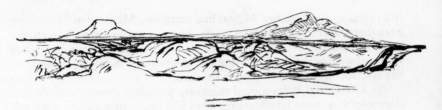

RENEGADE
XVII

"YOU knew Geronimo, Uncle Jimmie. What kind of man was he? What was he like?"

Without hesitation, Uncle Jimmie replied: "Geronimo was a liar. He lied to his own people as well as the whites. His people disliked and mistrusted him, but they feared him, too. Geronimo was a medicine man. His people believed he could make them sick or make them die if he wished. His following was never large, but he had much influence. Geronimo was a great talker and he was no coward. He claimed he could not be killed and his people believed him. But he was never a chief like Mangas Coloradas, Cochise or Victorio, who spoke the truth and were respected by their people. Geronimo was always a liar."

"Perhaps, he took a leaf from the white man's book," I said. Uncle Jimmie's bright eyes twinkled. "He even lied to me. It's a long story but it will show you what Geronimo was like—

"It was in 1882 when Geronimo raided my father's sheep camp near Ash Flat. My father, George Stevens, was born in Massachusetts. After the Civil War he came to Arizona as a trader and married my mother who was a Coyotero or White Mountain Apache. My father served the government in various capacities. He was the first sheriff of Graham County and we were living in Safford when Geronimo made his raid.

"Victoriano Mestas, a Mexican, was in charge of my father's sheep camp. He had been captured as a little boy by the Southern Chiricahuas and raised by the Apaches. Mestas had married a Mexican girl and there were three children. Bylas an Apache, who was my first cousin, with one of his wives and three of his children, was at the sheep camp, too, when an Apache came in with word that Geronimo and a big party of Chiricahua warriors were on their way to the camp.

So Mestas and Bylas moved the camp to higher ground and all that afternoon they made fortifications. They had plenty of guns and ammunition. Besides Mestas and Bylas, the Apache, there were ten Mexican herders. They posted guards that night and it was a few hours before daybreak when they heard a voice from the darkness:

" 'It is me, Mestas; it is Geronimo. I have many men and they are hungry. We will not harm you for I am Geronimo, your friend.'

" 'Don't let them in,' said Bylas, 'or they will kill you.' And Bylas taunted Geronimo. 'You lie, Geronimo, you want to kill us. Always you are a liar.' "

"Geronimo ignored Bylas, always he called from the darkness to Mestas. 'I have many men and we are hungry. We go to San Carlos to take our people back to Mexico. We will not harm you for I am your friend.'

" 'Don't let them in,' said Bylas, 'or they will kill you.'

"Again Geronimo called to Mestas: 'Many times have we drunk tulapai together. My people are hungry. We will not harm you for I am Geronimo, your friend.'

" 'Don't let them come in,' said Bylas. 'But Geronimo once gave me a pony an' saddle,' said Mestas. 'That was a long time ago,' said Bylas. 'You were living with the Chiricahuas then. Now you work for the white man, George Stevens. Don't let them come in for they will kill you.'

"But after it grew light Mestas allowed Geronimo and his band to come in. First they posted the Mexican herders with their guns and Bylas ordered them to be on their guard and not mix with the Chiricahuas. There were seventy-six in Geronimo's band. Nachee, the son of Cochise, was there and Chato and Chihuahua. Mestas' wife cooked tortillas for the whole band.

"The Chiricahuas killed many of my father's sheep. Some of the sheep they gouged their eyes out and did not kill. And Geronimo killed a two-year-old sorrel colt that belonged to me. Geronimo liked horse meat, he did not like mutton to eat.

"While the Chiricahuas were eating and joking, they joked with the Mexican herders who grew careless. Then, at a signal from Geronimo, the Chiricahuas disarmed the herders and tied their hands behind their backs. They tied Mestas—first Geronimo made Mestas take off his shirt, it was a Mexican shirt with much embroidery; Geronimo wanted the pretty shirt and he did not want it bloody. And when Mestas' wife had finished cooking tortillas they tied her up with two of the children. But Mestas' little son was standing by Bylas' woman and she hid the little boy beneath her skirts.

"Nachee, the son of Cochise, and Chato sat talking to Bylas who spoke to Geronimo: 'Why do you want to kill these people after they have fed you and you promised to harm no one?' They would have killed Bylas, too, if it had not been for Nachee.

" 'Don't talk so much,' said Nachee, 'or Geronimo will get mad. Let me do the talking. You have plenty of money, Geronimo, why don't you pay Mestas' woman for the tortillas she cooked?'

"Then Chato spoke: 'Why do you want to kill these people when you promised to do them no harm? We would have lost many men had we tried to attack the camp.'

"Geronimo said nothing but Chihuahua then spoke and he was a bad one. 'These people are Mexicans and they are our enemies. Always the Mexicans have lied to us and killed our people.'

" 'These people have not lied to you,' said Nachee, 'they have fed us. Why don't you pay Mestas' woman who cooked for us?' 'These people are Mexicans, they are our enemies,' said Chihuahua. 'we will kill them.'

"So they ran a long rope through the thongs that bound each prisoner's hands behind their back and led them up the hill a little way from the camp. And the Chiricahuas shot and stabbed till all were dead—the herders, Mestas, his wife and the two little children; they butchered them all. There was one Mexican herder who slipped the rope and ran but he did not get far before he was shot down. And while they were shooting at him, they nearly hit Geronimo who ran back to where Nachee and Chato sat with Bylas.

" 'Here he comes,' said Nachee, 'and he is mad; if he says anything we will kill him.' Nachee spoke to his two nephews: 'If Geronimo says a word, kill him.' Geronimo heard what Nachee said and he did not speak.

"In the meantime Mestas' little son had crawled out from under Bylas' woman's skirts. 'Hoo,' said a Chiricahua, 'here's one we missed.' 'Kill him, too,' said Geronimo.

"That was when the Chiricahua warrior threatened Geronimo. This warrior was a Mexican who had been captured as a little boy and raised by the Chiricahuas. He was a small man but he was a great warrior and very brave. Seizing a spear he held it at Geronimo's heart as he spoke: 'I am a warrior, Geronimo, always I have obeyed your orders. The people you have killed today are my people but something—I think it is their God—has spared the little one's life. Do not harm him or I will kill you, Geronimo.' Then the Mexican who was raised as a Chiricahua warrior faced the entire band: 'I will kill any man who harms the little boy. You are many, I am alone, but I will take many with me when I go.'

"That was how Mestas' little son was saved, he was the only one for Geronimo and the Chiricahuas knew the Mexican was very brave. Bylas' woman led Mestas' little boy away and cared for him. The rest of the Mexicans were later buried in a common grave. You have been to Geronimo Springs? Then, without knowing, you have rode by the grave. Bylas was my first cousin; it was Bylas who told me the story."

"You said Geronimo lied to you, Uncle Jimmie?"

"He did and it was about my sorrel pony he killed that day. It was many years later, at the Omaha Exposition in 1898. I was in charge of the San Carlos Apaches who were there; I had thirty-two tickets, including my own. Geronimo was there and Nachee and many Chiricahuas who had been deported from Arizona. They lived in a camp by themselves but Captain Mercer, who was in charge of all Indians at the Exposition, gave Nachee and his family permission to come and camp with us since Nachee had relatives among the San Carlos Apaches.

"Geronimo often came to our camp and we had many talks. He thought because I was in charge of the San Carlos Apaches I was a "big-shot" and might help him get back to Arizona. Geronimo was always talking about coming back to Arizona.

"Once when we were talking alone he told me of a cave in the Sierra Madre mountains in Old Mexico where a fortune in gold and silver bars was hidden. Geronimo's band had wiped out a Mexican pack train. Many guns and much ammunition was in the cave, too. The gold and silver bars and the guns and ammunition had been covered with raw-hide, then it had all been covered with rocks and boulders. 'Jimmie,' said Geronimo, 'if you will use your influence to get me back to Arizona I will take you to the cave in the Sierra Madres and all the gold and silver will be yours.'

"When I told Nachee what Geronimo had told me, Nachee laughed; he didn't discount the cave or the fortune in gold and silver bars. 'He will take you to the cave in the Sierra Madres,' said Nachee, 'but you will never come back. Geronimo will kill you for he is always a liar.' Nachee, the son of Cochise, was tall, over six feet and slender. Geronimo was not so tall but always he was restless and full of energy."

"Why was Nachee, the son of Cochise, dominated by Geronimo?"

"He wasn't," said Uncle Jimmie. "Nachee was married into Geronimo's family and those ties are very close to an Apache. But Nachee was not afraid of Geronimo, he was not afraid of anyone. I saw him laugh in Geronimo's face. That was when General Miles and Geronimo had their big talk at the Exposition.

"The officials at the Exposition thought it would be a fine thing for

Geronimo and General Miles to talk as Geronimo had surrendered to
General Miles at Skeleton Canyon in 1886. But General Miles refused to
talk unless I interpreted for him, he didn't trust Geronimo's interpreter.
When the General asked me if I'd interpret, I said Yes, if Geronimo
would pay me for a horse he owed me. I told General Miles about the
sorrel colt Geronimo had killed an' eaten at my father's sheep camp in
1882. So we put it up to Geronimo. He asked what I wanted for the colt.
Fifty dollars, I said.

" 'It's too much for the colt,' said Geronimo, 'an' besides, I don't
have that much money.'

"That was when Geronimo lied to me for he had just told me that
the day before he had made sixty-four dollars selling postcards. Geronimo
had learned to print his name in roman numerals and he sold signed post-
card-pictures of himself for a dollar a piece." Uncle Jimmie laughed.
"Geronimo never did pay me for the pony but it was worth fifty dollars
to look at his face when I interpreted for General Miles.

"That was a big day at the Exposition. Many people were gathered
to hear General Miles and Geronimo talk, Geronimo was to speak first.
He was a great talker but his hand trembled and he broke out in a sweat
and stuttered, at first he could not speak. That was when Nachee laughed
in his face.

" 'Speak,' said Nachee, 'for years you have told us what you would
say to General Miles if the chance ever came. Now you sweat, Geronimo,
and your hand trembles; you are afraid, Geronimo.' And once more
Nachee laughed in his face.

"But Geronimo didn't do so bad when he got started for he was a
great talker. Of course, I have forgotten much that was said since it was
a long time ago but it went about like this:

" 'The United States is a great country,' said Geronimo, 'and you,
General Miles, are a great man since you are a general in the army.
When we surrendered to you in Skeleton Canyon in Arizona you said we
would see our families in Florida within five days; you said that all was
forgiven. You lied to us, General Miles, for you sent us to an island in
Florida where many of our people sickened and died; you lied to us, General Miles. In Arizona the quail, the deer and the turkey miss Geronimo.
The mountains miss him.' " Uncle Jimmie laughed again. "There was
much more to the same effect, Geronimo spoke for a long time. When he
had finished, General Miles replied.

" 'I did lie to you, Geronimo, but I learned to lie from you, Geronimo, who is the greatest of all liars. When I lied I saved your life, Geronimo, for had you remained in Arizona the citizens of the Territory would have hung you for your crimes. The quail, the deer, the turkey and the mountains do not miss you, Geronimo, nor do the people in Arizona miss you; for those who follow the lonely trails and live in lonely places sleep soundly now, knowing that you, Geronimo, are far from Arizona and will not butcher them.' No, General Miles didn't do so bad, either, what he said took the wind out of Geronimo, too.

"A while back," said Uncle Jimmie, "you said something about Geronimo taking a leaf from the white man's book. Well, I guess he took several leaves from the book. Geronimo could not only lie as well as any white man, he was shrewd. He liked to make money and he was a good salesman, too. Aside from the signed picture-postcards he sold of himself for a dollar apiece, he made little bows and arrows that he sold for ten dollars.

"There was an Indian Commissioner from Washington, named Jones, at the Exposition; Geronimo made a flowery speech and presented the Commissioner with a bow and some arrows. I interpreted and one would have thought the Commissioner was a long-lost friend of Geronimo's. As a Commissioner from Washington, Jones could not be obligated to Geronimo and Geronimo knew this, too. The Commissioner asked me what Geronimo sold the bow and arrows for. When I said ten dollars, the Commissioner peeled a ten off his roll. Geronimo took, it, too; it was his way of making a sale.

"Can you imagine Geronimo getting lost?" said Uncle Jimmie. "I've known cowpunchers who got lost in town," I replied. "Well, Geronimo wasn't in town. When he got lost he was in the country and he was not alone, either. There were about fifteen of us together, all Apaches, and we were all lost.

"While we were in Omaha, nearly every Sunday we rode out and visited ranches in the country. The Apaches have always loved melons and squash to eat and the ranchers seldom charged us for anything. Nachee, the son of Cochise, was with us. All the ranchers had heard of Geronimo, they would ask him questions while I interpreted. Geronimo loved to talk and he was a good actor, too.

"On this particular Sunday there was no sun, it was a cloudy day. We

followed roads in many directions since that country is under fence. Did
you ever see that country? There is nothing but corn in that country as
far as the eye can see. We visited several ranches and had eaten many
melons and squash when we started back to town. We followed one road
for a while, then we would follow another. Finally we got lost. 'No mountains,' said Geronimo, 'nothing but corn in this damn country.'

"We knew we could find our way back if the stars came out but I
knew Captain Mercer would be worried. He was in charge of all Indians
at the Exposition and we were supposed to be back on the grounds by
dark. Finally I found a telephone at a ranch house and called Captain
Mercer; he was greatly relieved. We were almost twenty miles from
Omaha, Captain Mercer rode out and met us.

"It caused quite a stir in Omaha papers, too. Geronimo was always
talking to reporters about going back to Arizona. When he didn't come
in at dark they thought he and Nachee had pulled out and gone. For a
time Omaha had a real Indian scare, but Geronimo was only lost in the
corn."

It is ironical that Geronimo, who was without honor or integrity, even
among his own people, is the one Apache who is best known today. In the
late war, paratroopers screamed his name—"Geronimo"—as they unloaded from the sky.

A Southern Chiricahua, Geronimo was born about 1832; he died at
Fort Sill, Oklahoma, February 17, 1909. Had he remained in Arizona,
Geronimo would have been hung for the countless murders he committed.
Deported and shipped East in 1886, he lived for twenty-three years as a
prisoner of war. Nor was he destined to ever see again the mountains of
Arizona or the Sierra Madres (the Mother Mountains) of Old Mexico.
Only a mountain man can understand his punishment.

As a prisoner he was exploited by the government. It was a great
build-up for the old renegade and Geronimo, always the showman, loved
it. At the Expositions at Omaha, Buffalo, at the World's Fair in St. Louis,
he sold picture-postcards of himself, bows and arrows. Men and women
fawned upon him, shook his bloodstained hand. When Theodore Roosevelt was inaugurated President, it was Geronimo, on a paint pony, who
stole the show in the inaugural parade.

A few years before his death, Geronimo joined The Dutch Reformed

Church. It must be said, however, that he was never a regular attendant nor was there any apparent reformation.

Geronimo had driven into Lawton, Oklahoma, sold a bow and arrows, and bought a bottle of liquor. Driving back to the reservation he got drunk and fell out of the buggy. A cold rain was falling and he was not found for several hours; taken to the hospital, he died a few days later. His passing was not mourned in Arizona.

UNCLE JIMMIE SPEAKS:
XVIII

VICTORIO

"DID YOU know Victorio, Uncle Jimmie?"
"No, I didn't, but I was at my father's ranch when Victorio raided it, in 1880. I was eleven years old at the time. You have been to the old Double Circle Ranch? Then you know the place. My father, George Stevens, was the first man to locate that ranch.

"My father was away at the time of the raid but there was a white man, named Yank, at the ranch. That was all I ever heard him called. He had served with my father during the Civil War. The rest were Apaches. Bylas' father and his woman was there and Cooncan and his woman and there were others whose names I have forgotten. They had built their wickiups about the ranch house. From a distance it looked to be quite a village.

"The Apaches were sitting out in the yard when one of them happened to look across at the mountain. At first he thought it to be a bird flying but upon looking closer he saw it was an Indian on a running horse. As he watched, he saw more Indians on running horses and then they knew it was a raid. Indians were rounding up my father's horses and cattle.

"There were many chairs in front of the ranch house. Bylas' father placed them in a circle; he put blankets over the chairs so that from a great distance it looked as if they were holding a council. Shortly after this they saw a signal from the mountain asking for someone to come out and talk.

"An Apache woman went first; she said she was old, it made no difference if they killed her or not. After a long time she returned; she said they could not understand her and wanted someone else to come out. But she said the raiders were Warm Springs Apaches from New Mexico and Victorio was the chief. Then another Apache woman said she would

178

go. Her man was afraid but when his woman hid a knife in her skirts and started alone, he could do nothing but follow.

"As you know, my mother was a White Mountain or Coyotero Apache. She gave Yank a rifle and a belt of ammunition and it was my mother who planned to defend the ranch house. She told the Apaches what to do.

"My father had considerable money at the ranch, several thousand dollars in gold and paper money. My mother put it all in a big tin can. A cabin next to the ranch house had burned down; under the old chimney my mother buried the can. Then they built a fire over it. My mother called me to her:

" 'Jimmie,' she said, 'you are eleven years old and almost a man. There are five other children here. Take them to Fort Apache and tell the officer what is going on here.' And mother gave me a case knife she had sharpened. 'Keep it sharp on the rocks and keep it hidden; use the knife if they capture you, use it well and kill. They will kill you, then; that is better than being taken prisoner.' My mother was always very brave.

"I was barefoot and wearing only a shirt and underwear my mother had made for me. My mother told me how to go and we slipped into the brush. We had not gone far until we heard voices we could not understand. They were Indians but their headdress was something we had never seen before. We watched them pass as we hid in the brush. Later we found they were Comanches.

"After they passed us we went on again. Some time later we had stopped to rest when I saw moving shadows above us and I dove into the brush. Later I found it was our own people, come to take us back; they took the other children but I didn't know it at the time.

"I was alone now and it got dark. All that night I laid in the brush and I was hungry and cold. I didn't want to go to Fort Apache, I wanted to see my mother. I hid in the brush all day and that evening I slipped into the ranch.

"The sheep were in the corrals. At first I was going to put up the bars, then I knew there was no one to turn them out. It was dark when I slipped into the house and I was afraid. I went to the oven and found two loaves of bread my mother had baked. They had been left in the oven and were partly burned. I found jerky in the house but my mother and the Apaches were gone.

"For three days I hid in the brush, I did not go far from the ranch. Each night the sheep came into the corral, and there was no one to put up the bars. It was on the third night when I saw a little fire in a canyon and I crawled toward it. There were two Apache women with a blanket over their heads, a little fire to keep them warm. I crawled closer and touched one of the women. 'Don't kill,' she said, 'please don't kill me.' Then the other woman spoke: 'Who are you talking to?' 'Someone is touching me,' she said. Then I spoke: 'It is me, it is Jimmie. Is my mother alive?' 'Yes, she is alive,' they said, 'an' you will see her soon.'

"My mother put her arms about me and held me close. From my mother I learned what had happened. Yank had deserted us. Later we found he went to Fort Apache and told the soldiers we had all been killed by the raiders, that we were all dead. I never saw Yank again, my father would have nothing to do with Yank after he ran out on us.

"Knowing that they could not defend the ranch, my mother and the Apaches took to the brush and scattered. That was why I found the ranch deserted and was afraid my mother had been killed or carried off. But the woman who put the knife in her skirt, and whose husband did not want to go with her, saw Victorio. He did not know it was my father's ranch he had raided.

" 'When I was at San Carlos,' said Victorio, 'George Stevens was my friend. We have taken his horses and cattle and I am sorry. But there are Comanches with us on the raid. I have promised them horses and cattle.

I can do nothing about it. But George Stevens was my friend at San
Carlos and I am sorry.'

"They did not bother my father's sheep or the ranch house. They
took only horses and cattle. Nor did Victorio kill our people. He was not
like Geronimo who would have killed us all just for the hell of it."

COCHISE

"COCHISE called my mother Sister," said Uncle Jimmie. "She was
not his sister, I don't know what the relationship was. It may have
been what you call a forty-second cousin but blood ties mean much
to an Apache. My father was a white man but Cochise called him
Brother and Cochise once saved my father's life.

"My father was carrying mail for the government from Fort Buchanan
to Fort Bowie when it happened. He had certain camps where he always
stopped but something had gone wrong with the buckboard so he stopped
to fix it. He had stopped on the water so he cooked dinner, too, and he
was making bread when he saw Apaches approaching. There were about
twenty in the band and they were so close when he saw them he knew it
was no use to go for his rifle.

"Then my father saw that Cochise was in the lead. Cochise carried
a Winchester in the crook of his left arm and he carried a six-shooter that
was tied with a buckskin thong to his right wrist. Cochise dismounted and

said: 'My Brother, you are supposed to be dead!' Cochise told my father
what had happened. Some Apaches had come from New Mexico to kill
my father; I don't know why, unless it was because he was a white man
and was married to an Apache woman. But Cochise got wind of the
affair and he rode hard to the water where my father usually camped.
And Cochise and his warriors attacked the Apaches who were waiting to
kill my father. The leader escaped; some Apaches, Cochise and his men
killed, and there were two prisoners they had taken who were tied on a
horse.

"The Chiricahuas dragged the two Apache prisoners from the horse
and Cochise handed my father a spear. 'Kill them,' said Cochise, 'for
they are your enemies and have tried to kill you.' When my father hesi-
tated, Cochise handed him his Winchester, thinking my father did not
want to use the spear. 'Shoot them' said Cochise, 'for they are your
enemies and have tried to kill you.'

"Then my father spoke: 'I do not want to kill them; I am married to
an Apache woman and all Apaches are my friends.' Cochise found this
hard to understand but he released the two prisoners when my father refused to kill them.

"Years later, in New Mexico, the two Apaches whom Cochise had
taken prisoner came and spoke to my father and were very grateful that
he had not killed them. They became my father's friends."

PINE TREE

"THERE were Indians at Omaha from all over the country," said
Uncle Jimmie. "And there was a Blackfoot from Montana who
fell in love with an Apache girl from San Carlos, Arizona. They
came to me with a hundred dollars to give the girl's mother at San Carlos;
the Apache girl said she loved this Blackfoot and was going back to Montana with him. I had promised the Apaches at San Carlos I would bring
all their people back and I said 'No'. When I told Captain Mercer, who
was in charge of all Indians, he said the Apache girl could not go to Montana with this Blackfoot. So that settled it or, at least, we thought it did.

"We called the Blackfeet 'them striped Indians' because of the striped coats they wore and we called this Blackfoot who was in love with the Apache girl 'Pine Tree', he was so tall. Miles Big Spring was his name.

"When the Blackfoot train pulled out for Montana, Pine Tree was on the train but he got off the train at Lincoln and walked back to Omaha. That is a long walk even for an Indian. The first I knew about it was when someone came to me and said, 'Pine Tree is here again.' Pine Tree was crying, too; he said he loved the girl so much he wanted to go to San Carlos with her. When I told Captain Mercer, he said, 'Well, if he loves the girl that much, let him go.'

"After we got back to San Carlos, Pine Tree sent for me to come and see him, he said he was in trouble. When I asked him what his trouble was, he told me his woman had made the tepee too small, his feet were outside when he slept." Uncle Jimmie laughed. "So I told Pine Tree's woman to make the tepee bigger. There was really no trouble between them, they loved each other very much."

There is a sequel to the story of Pine Tree and the Apache girl. Twenty-nine years later, in 1927, my friend, Lone Wolf, the Blackfoot artist, came to see me in Globe, Arizona. "Will you go with me to San Carlos?" said Lone Wolf. "Miles Big Spring, one of my people, is living there. His father who lives in Montana is very old and would like to see him." Then Lone Wolf told how Miles Big Spring had fallen in love with the Apache girl and how he came to Arizona.

"Miles and I are about the same age," said Lone Wolf. "As boys we played together on the reservation in Montana and we were about eight years old when soldiers rounded us up, along with many other Blackfoot children, and we were sent to school at Fort Shaw. It was in the dead of winter and very cold when they loaded us into the wagons to take us away. None of us wanted to go nor did our people want us to go. Many of them were crying, too, that morning when we were taken away.

"At Fort Shaw the soldiers took all our belongings from us, little medicine bags given us by our mothers. They took everything we had, piled it up in a heap and burned it. They cut our hair which was a disgrace to us and we were put in school with the Crows, who were our hereditary enemies. My uncle was about eighteen, he was sent with us, too. But my uncle had been on the war trail and he didn't stay very long. Many of the older boys ran away but there was nothing for the little ones, like Miles and myself, to do but take it.

"Well, some time before we were taken to Fort Shaw, I had found an illustrated magazine; it was the first magazine I had ever seen. All the drawings and paintings I'd seen before were on skins—flat, Indian designs with no perspective. Of course, I didn't know what perspective was but the magazine opened up a new world for the drawings were alive to me. I had loaned the magazine to Miles Big Spring; Miles liked pictures, too, and he had taken the magazine with him. The soldiers burned it; it was hard to keep the tears back as I watched it go up in smoke.

"We studied from a chart in school. If it was a picture of a cow, we spelled it out as the teacher pointed to each letter; then we pronounced the word 'cow'. Well, Miles would spell out the words but he would not pronounce them. If it was a picture of cow, Miles would spell it out but he would pronounce it 'dog' or, mebbe, he would call it 'horse'. I don't know why he did it, he knew better. Even when he was punished, he refused to pronounce the right word."

Like his friend, Miles Big Spring, whom the Apaches called 'Pine Tree', Lone Wolf is tall and slender, well over six feet. Down on the reservation we stopped some Apache cowboys to inquire where Miles Big Spring's tepee was located. "Your people," said one, and Lone Wolf nodded.

Miles Big Spring remembered the friend of his boyhood but he had forgotten his own language. Nor would he go back to Montana. "I have the money with me and your father is old," said Lone Wolf. Miles Big Spring did not look at his friend, he was watching a distant peak when he finally replied: "The time has been long and I would like to see my

father. But my family is here; I have children and grandchildren now, here is where I belong."

He asked Lone Wolf to count for him, to speak to him in his own tongue hoping it might come back. Slowly, almost halting, he repeated the words as Lone Wolf spoke and slowly their meaning came. After all, twenty-nine years is a long time.

APACHE KID

"YOU knew the Apache Kid, Uncle Jimmie?"

"Yes, I knew him well. Kid gave me five dollars once. It was when the Wright brothers were killed. Some Apache renegades had run off horses that belonged to the Wrights. When the brothers followed, they were ambushed and killed. You know the place; it's not far from where the highway goes through today.

"We were living in Solomonville when the Apache Police from San Carlos came through on the trail of the renegades. Kid was along for he was a policeman although he was very young. He stopped and talked to me for we were friends and had often played together. 'Jimmie', he said, 'here's five dollars, for you are still going to school and I am a policeman now'. Kid was all right, everyone liked him until he got into trouble."

As Uncle Jimmie and I talked in front of the Trading Post, he pointed to a squaw, old and wrinkled; she was the Kid's sister.

"Uncle Jimmie, did you ever know what happened to the Mexican who was captured by the Apaches as a little boy and became a great Chiricahua warrior—I mean the one who held the spear at Geronimo's heart that day at your father's sheep camp?"

"I asked Geronimo about him in Omaha," said Uncle Jimmie. "He was killed in a fight in Old Mexico; Geronimo said he was very brave."

"You were a cowpuncher," said Uncle Jimmie. "Horse wrangler," I said. Uncle Jimmie laughed. "Anyway, they are all alike. Did I tell you about the cowpuncher we met coming back from Omaha?

"Our train had stopped at La Junta, Colorado, and a soldier said—'Hello, Jimmie, what are you doin' up here?'. At first I didn't know him; the last time I had seen him he wore cowboy clothes and we had gone to enlist in the Rough Riders together and I was turned down.

"Well, this cowpuncher had been discharged. He had got drunk an' gone broke with some cowpunchers from Colorado and he was trying to get back to Arizona. I told him I thought I could get him back on the train with us. We had an Apache baby with us so I scratched the baby's name off the ticket and wrote the cowpuncher's name instead.

"When the conductor came into our car he saw the soldier in uniform and said: 'You are in the wrong car; this car is for Apaches going to Arizona.' 'I am Mr. Stevens' assistant, in charge of these Indians,' said the soldier. 'Mr. Stevens has the tickets.'

"When the conductor came to me he counted the Indians and the tickets. 'There is a baby,' he said. 'Well, you don't charge an Apache baby,' I said, 'any more than you do a white baby.' The conductor took the tickets and said nothing more. That was how the cowpuncher got back to Arizona."

"So you were turned down for the Rough Riders?" I said.

"They said I had a bad heart," said Uncle Jimmie.

"And you are seventy-six now?"

"Almost seventy-seven," said Uncle Jimmie; "and many who were taken are gone and I am still alive."

A faraway look came into Uncle Jimmie's eyes. He was not thinking of the Rough Riders. Uncle Jimmie was thinking of his own sons in the late war, of one who did not come back.

WRANGLING

XIX

WRANGLING horses and hunting for lost ponies on the range was a pain in the neck to most cowpunchers, yet it was a chore I always enjoyed. I liked it even better when the roundup wasn't on. It gave me a chance to prowl alone; there was never any hurry and aside from the lost ponies, there were other things I found.

Ruins built by an ancient people were common on the range, so common in fact as to go unnoticed by most punchers. There were manos and metates often lying about that had been used for grinding corn long before Columbus sailed, and there were always the broken bits of pottery, often with figures painted in beautiful design. When we cleaned out the spring at the old Bar F Bar headquarters we found bits of turquoise, beads and shells, offerings of the ancients to their water gods by a people long since gone. Scooping out a seep spring with my hands on Mescal so the pony and I could water out, I found two pieces of pierced turquoise and a necklace of sea shells.

In Saw Mill canyon on the upper range there were caves, their roofs still black with smoke where ancients at one time dwelt, where I found reed arrows tipped with hardwood points and sandals made of bear

187

grass. There were cliff dwellings in Saw Mill canyon, too; some inaccessible, others, however, where corncobs and pieces of squash and pumpkin shell were so well preserved it was hard to believe they were over two years old.

Hunting horses with Ole Indian Jim one day, he pointed to an ancient ruin and said: "Long time ago my house!" "What do you know about it, Jim?" Jim spread his hands and raised his eyes; it was the gesture he always used whenever he didn't know. Nor did any old Apache I ever questioned know any more about the ancients who had come and gone than I did, and my knowledge still is nil.

There was a rifle pit I found one day on a little butte. Real work had been done on it, too. From the way the rocks had been arranged and piled, it had taken several hours to build it. The pit was big enough to hold two or three men comfortably. Scattered about the floor of the pit were one hundred and fifty-odd empty shells, green and mouldy with age. I packed a couple into the ranch, cleaned them enough to identify them as .45-90 shells. But none of the old punchers had any knowledge of the rifle pit, nor could they recall any fight that had taken place.

There was the barrel of an old muzzle-loader, a smooth bore, I found by a seep spring underneath Mescal rim and a part of a rifle with much brass I carried in that was identified by the old punchers as simply a "yellow-belly."

"Wonder what he's got this time?" Old Ed would say. "He's worse than ary pack rat."

But as for the "yellow-belly" rifle, I learned it was not so ancient. We were trying to clean it enough to identify the gun when Buck B., one of the old punchers, happened by. "Hell," he said, "I burnt up one of them things once, shootin' at the soldiers." That was all the information he volunteered, nor did we ask him questions. It was only on rare occasions that Old Buck spoke about his past.

A stray puncher had left a newspaper several weeks old at our camp. That night by the fire I read the paper aloud to Buck whose eyes were none too good. There was a copy of Governor Hunt's speech, the Governor was running for reelection and it was easy to tell by Old Buck's sniffs and snorts that he was not altogether in sympathy with the Governor's politics. When the Governor, in the course of his remarks, stated that he had been afoot when he first entered the Territory over forty years before,

Old Buck declared himself. "That's nothin' to brag about," said Buck. "I was afoot myself when I first landed here." Then Old Buck went so far as to say that a sheriff had shot a horse from under him just before he crossed the line.

There were two little piles of rock, miles from each other and far from any trail, that marked lonely graves on the range. Not far from one I found the little wooden cross, but there was no identification on it. And

there was the little wooden cross I found one day while fixing a water gap; the cross was lodged in the drift and had come down when the wash ran. "Killed by Apaches"—that was all, nor did I ever find the grave.

One shipping day on Cutter Flat the wrangler brought into camp a piece of an old ox shoe. "There's probably a lot more scattered about," Jimmy Gibson said. "They used to winter oxen here fifty years ago."

One was forever riding on to the monuments put up by the prospectors with the location notice in the tin can. On one location I found the can was rotting away. Nor could the location notice inside the can be read, it was yellow and faded with age. Why the old-timer had located the ground was a puzzle, too; as far as I could see there was no sign of any mineral. But knowing little about such things I had an old prospector ride with me one day. Nor could he figure it out. "There ain't no mineral within ten miles of here," he said, "but some of these old boys go queer. Chances are this old-timer put his marker up simply because he had nothin' else to do, then again the old boy might have believed he was locatin' something worth while; really believed it, too, figgered he had located something he could sell for at least a million dollars."

The old cowpunchers usually figured if they were not killed when a horse turned over on them, they'd wind up at some headquarters "waitin' on the ranch." Not so the old prospector; the hole in the ground he sat upon might not even be good rock, but as far as the old prospector went, that hole in the ground was worth all of a million dollars.

Most prospectors didn't want visitors snooping around; they hadn't always done their assessment work, but a cowboy on a horse was something else again. They knew the average waddie wouldn't get off a horse long enough to dig a hole in the ground.

Bob Henry and Guy Smith, long since gone to their reward, had some claims on Silver Creek on the western end of the range. It was always good to ride their way. They had a garden, I'll never forget the lettuce and radishes or the fried chicken and sweet corn those two old boys put out. It was a real change from a straight diet of beef and frijole beans. They had a milk cow, a Bar F Bar cow they had gentled; while the waddies who worked for the outfit got their milk from cans.

Neither Bob nor Guy slipped any joints in a frenzy of labor. They would take off the day and the night, too, any time one of us happened by. One morning as I was leaving for the ranch with the coming of the morning star, both old-timers walked with me to where my pony stood. "Come again," said Bob, "an' make it soon. Me an' Guy aint spoke to each other in ten days till you rode in this morning." Then both old-timers slapped each other on the back and laughed. And there was Professor Buckland.

In his late seventies, he was as active as a cat and he had the bleached-blue eyes of so many of his kind. But the Professor spoke in clipped sentences; he was a learned man and the Professor loved to talk. He had been in the diamond fields of South Africa, he had gone over Chilkoot Pass in Alaska, too. When one of the punchers told him that I had "drawed pictures in a magazine," the Professor was not surprised but he never did mention it to me or fish around for stray bits of information that he might piece together. Like some of the old punchers, the Professor simply figured that I was wanted some place or else I wouldn't be wrangling horses.

Usually on a trip to town I packed a piece of beef in front of me;

from little things we'd observed, the Professor's rations were skimpy. On one trip I packed him a quarter, helped him jerk the meat. "Goodness, goodness, boy," he said, "there's enough meat on that jerky line to last me three whole months."

Nor was my head ever too heavy on leaving town to bring him the latest papers and magazines and they were always left casually. The Professor was a sensitive man. Some of us were good boys, he said. While the Professor never said so in as many words, he didn't think much of the cowpunchers as a breed. As a matter of fact, had he told the truth, he looked on the average waddie with no more respect than he would look at something that had crawled out from under a rock.

The Professor fell out with me one day when I attempted a joke; it was a feeble effort and I have always regretted it. I was on my way to the ranch from town and had a bottle with me. Why the bartender had given me Scotch instead of Bourbon is something I'll never know. As a matter of fact, it was the first time I ever tasted Scotch whiskey in my life; but the Professor was greatly pleased. I was given a dissertation on how whiskey was made, whiskey for gentlemen. The Professor really preferred Irish whiskey but Scotch was next in line and I was also given a lecture on how badly cowboys drank. Good whiskey should be sipped and tasted, never gulped and swallowed or put down the hatch as if a man were trying to drown a rat. There was a little left in the bottle when the Professor excused himself; he was only gone a few minutes when he returned with a cigar box full of specimens from a hidden cache outside.

The specimens were rich in gold and had been picked, probably carried and cherished by the Professor lo these many years. Even to my clouded eye the nuggets danced and shone. I looked each specimen over carefully and, trying to be facetious, I casually remarked: "Do these rocks carry any mineral?" For almost a full minute the Professor froze, sucking in his breath. At his first blast I would not have been surprised had the roof gone off the cabin. "Gold," he said, "it's gold!" Then he sputtered again, "Any damn fool, except a cowboy, would not ask such a simple question."

I said I was only fooling but the Professor would not be soothed. Always before on my visits he walked with me to my pony, and shook hands before I mounted. But when I left, the Professor simply gave me a curt "good-day," and slammed the cabin door.

A month later when I stopped with a piece of beef, he was civil—
that was all. I still continued to bring papers and magazines as if nothing
had ever happened; he always thanked me courteously. But never again
did the Professor invite me inside his little cabin.

When I spoke to Old Ed about it, the old puncher was surprised that
I had let the incident bother me. "Why, the Professor's loco," said Old
Ed; "you should have knowed it, too. All prospectors go nuts in time. It's
from bein' alone too much, they have too much time to think. Some
cowboys go nuts, too. It's a rare thing when it happens to a puncher,
though." Old Ed laughed. "I guess it's because we don't have enough on
our minds that it bothers us to think."

There was the lost mine in the R. S. pasture. Occasionally, an old
prospector and his burro dropped in to spend the night in his quest for it.
However, most of the ones who came were dudes from town on rented
saddle horses. We came to know their mission when we saw them riding
in. They asked us guarded questions—"Did any of the boys, when riding,
ever see a brass kettle in a tree?" It was supposed to be a mesquite, the
tree had grown until the kettle was buried in it. There was a "raster,"
too, that either the Spaniards or Mexicans had built for crushing ore.

All of the punchers knew the location of the brass kettle and of the
"raster," yet there was no sign of any mine or mineral; cowpunchers had
combed the place. When questioned, no puncher to my knowledge ever
committed himself. Yes, they had heard of the brass kettle in the tree
and of the "raster," too, but no puncher had ever found it!

When one of Old Ed's friends came out from town in his quest for
the lost mine he got no further than the rest. Later, I asked Ed why he
hadn't taken his friend to the place. Ed laughed. "If I showed him the
place, in a week's time hunters would be here an' underfoot in droves.
You know durn well, yourself, there's no mineral in that country. Let
'em find the place themselves."

The outfit was camped at the Big Corral. One evening as I rode into
headquarters with the pack mules for a load of chuck, I could hardly
believe my eyes. There was a buckboard at the saddle rack, still standing
on four wheels. Ed said it was the first rig to be driven to the ranch in
ten years since the road had all washed out. Anyway, they had made it
and the rig was in one piece.

Our guests were father and son, the man well past middle age, the son in his early thirties. Up to a certain point they were talkative. They were from California, had rented the rig in town. The old man asked the usual guarded questions. When he made no reference to the "raster" or the brass kettle in the tree, we knew it wasn't our lost mine they hunted and both Ed and I were interested.

"Didn't the old stage road used to go down the creek about two miles south of the ranch house?" Old Ed nodded his head. "Isn't there a big corral about four miles from the ranch house where the main creek was joined?" Old Ed said yes and, furthermore, the outfit was camping there right now. The stranger said there was a dobie house inside the corral— it had been an old stage station—and he stated, further, an older brother had cooked at the station over thirty years before. Ed said he'd helped on two occasions to rebuild the corral, but if there had been a dobie house inside the corral all traces of it were gone. But the stranger and his son were satisfied; next morning at daybreak they rode back to camp with me.

They carried a pick and shovel, they turned their livery horses into the remuda and left our camp on foot, nor did they ask any questions. They stayed three days; each morning when they left our camp they took a southeast course and did not return until dark. Naturally, we were curious as to what the strangers hunted and among ourselves we did considerable speculating. If it was a lost mine—hell, let 'em hunt. But, mebbe, the old man's brother had really cached some gold! Why not hold them up? There was much more to the same effect; we even worked out the holdup in detail, but all in fun, of course. It was a new topic of conversation. Each evening when the strangers came in they volunteered no information, nor did we ask them questions.

On the third night the old man was very tired when they came in. He said they had given it up. Would I take them to the ranchhouse. They wanted to get an early start for town in the morning, they were afraid they might get lost. I had already chunked the fire and put on the coffee-pot before Ed crawled out of his soogans. "Any luck?" asked Ed. The old man shook his head, but over the coffee he talked at quite some length. "I think we were close," he said. "It was a dobie corral and while you have replaced it with a cedar corral, I'm sure it was the place."

"Hell," said Ed, "you passed that place coming up the creek, not far from the 5 L Ranch. The brush has growed so much you probably drove within ten feet of the place an' never even seen it. You dod-dumned fellers that hunts for things always out-foxes yourselves. Why didn't you say it was an old dobie corral with a old, ruined dobie inside it? I'll tell you exactly where that place is." And Ed described it in detail. "If you can't find it, any 5 L cowpuncher will take you to the place."

They thanked us next morning when they left. But as to what they were really hunting, and if they ever found it, we never did find out.

Most of the old cowpunchers who rode in Apache Land thirty years ago were Texans. Ed had gone up the trail his first trip when he was just sixteen, when there wasn't a wire fence from the Gulf of Mexico as far north as a man could ride. He had been a Texas Ranger in the early '8o's. The only boast I ever heard him make was that he had never killed a man.

Old George had been raised near San Antonio. Puny and suffering from asthma, he had been sent as a boy to an uncle in New Mexico. In a running fight between cowboys and Apaches, George had killed his first Indian when he was only twelve years old. "I lifted his hair, too," said George, "scalped the son of a —. Course, I couldn't tell this to just everybody, they wouldn't understand. But it was the custom among cowpunchers then to lift an Indian's hair."

Whatever the bugs George had when he left San Antonio were evidently eaten up by alkali dust in New Mexico and later in Arizona. George was almost ninety when he took his last long ride. He was in good health and spirits, too, until he got a little drunker than common, fell down and broke his shoulder and laid out for several hours. Taken to the hospital, pneumonia carried him off.

One old cowboy I worked with had come in with John Slaughter, who founded the San Bernardino ranch, and not only fought Apaches but Mexican bandits as well. The old puncher said he'd rather fight a dozen Sonora bandits any day than one Apache Indian.

And there was Henry Hooker who founded his empire—the Sierra Bonita Ranch was known to many famous people. Augustus Thomas was a guest and later wrote "Arizona," one of the popular plays of its day.

Bill Sparks, an old friend, wet-nursed Frederic Remington on one trip when that great artist was in Apache Land. As a boy with his uncle, Bill had hunted buffalo on the plains, later he gathered buffalo bones; at sixteen he went to Dodge City from Texas with a trail herd. As a professional hunter on Blue River in Arizona he sold wild turkeys, bear meat

and venison to the mining camp at Clifton. A sergeant in the Arizona
Rangers, Bill later went to Cuba with the Carter P. Johnson Expedition.
Later he was a packer in the Philippines.

Bill one day admitted to me that there was nothing he ever tried he
couldn't do, until he met Frederic Remington. "I used to look over his
shoulder when he drew," said Bill, "figgered I might learn the knack of
it myself. One day Fred got fed up. 'Here's paper and pencil, Bill,' he
says. 'Now go ahead and draw.' Ya know," said Bill, "it was the first
thing I ever tried I couldn't do. But those little pencil sketches Fred
made, them little things he sat an' scratched of Mexican steers and cow
ponies with drooping heads; well, they didn't mean much to me until I
saw his painting of 'The Trail Herd.' Then all them little things he
wooled about—a critter's hocks, a pony's legs—well, in that picture of
'The Trail Herd' all of that messin' around he done had finally come
alive."

There was Pete Kitchen, too. That old mus-hog, gone long before my
time, who is still a legend in Arizona. Pete had his own private cemetery
only a few miles from where Nogales stands today. Pete was one of the
few ranchers of his time the Apaches could never dislodge. They killed
his herders and his stock, they killed his stepson; but old Pete would not
be whipped. Nor did Pete die looking down a rifle barrel. Pete died in
bed, and peacefully, when our Good Lord set his time.

And there was a man named Smith, with two partners, whom the Apaches attacked one morning at daybreak at Pantano Wash. His partners were both killed at the first fire but Smith fought on alone; with a shotgun he killed so many Apaches and fought with such ferocity, the Indians finally withdrew and left him alone to bury his dead partners. And to the day he died, to distinguish him from others of his tribe who carried the name, he was known as Shotgun Smith.

On day herd one day an old waddie casually remarked to me that he had been a packer for General Crook. "What was he like?" I asked. The old waddie pondered at some length before he spoke. "General Crook knowed more about pack mules than ary packer in his outfit." Talking at any length was a lost art with many of the old-timers.

And there was another old friend. Bob's not his name but it will do, nor will I give his partner's name. While both old-timers are gone, there are grandchildren who might underestimate two salty old grandpappies. Bob, a waspy little man from Missouri, was said to have brought one of the first herds of cattle into Gila County. He located his ranch at Grapevine Springs on Salt River where Roosevelt Lake is today. He was alone and cooking dinner when a stranger rode into the ranch. The stranger wore a pith helmet, wore an old suit of linen clothes, even wore leather knee-pads that aroused the cowman's curiosity. "What the hell a man in this country wanted leather knee-pads for," said Bob, "had me up a tree. The stranger rode a mule, and instead of a rifle in the saddle boot he had a shotgun slung to the pommel. He didn't introduce himself, nor did I ask any questions—it wasn't the custom of the country.

"He refused the jug I passed him, polite of course, but I took several snorts myself. Intelligent he was, too, about things we talked about, although he never committed himself. When he left he thanked me for the meal, remarked how well I fed. 'It's simple,' I says, 'my pardner, Artie, is in the commissary at San Carlos; he sends the chuck here by the wagonload—flour, sugar, canned goods, all our horseshoes, too. There aint nothin' the Army issues that we don't have at the ranch.'

"A few days later one of the neighbors dropped in an' said that General Crook was in the country. I was curious to see him, too, so I caught up a saddle horse an' we contacted the cavalry column. I saw this old coot with his helmet an' linen duster ridin' on his mule in the middle of the column. To me he was just a coffee-cooler who had throwed in with the soldiers. But when I asked an officer to point out General Crook to me— Yep, you guessed it right, the General had been my guest! Why the General wore knee-pads still puzzled me but the officer said General Crook was a great hunter, he was forever on his knees when he was stalking game.

"A funny thing about it—General Crook's visit at my place got me in trouble, too. He preferred charges against Artie, my pardner, for government goods we stole. I've always been sorry about it; that is, about the way I talked that day when the General dropped in on me. You know, I had to go into court and perjure myself before I got my pardner cleared."

Many of the young officers who won their spurs in Apache Land later became well known. Lawton, Wood and Chaffee, just to mention a few. And as a shavetail out of West Point, one of John J. Pershing's first assignments was chasing a renegade Apache who was known as Geronimo. Two of the most promising young officers killed were Lt. Howard B. Cushing and Capt. Emmet Crawford. Lieutenant Cushing was killed when his little band was ambushed by Chiricahuas under their chief, Cochise. The gallant Crawford met his death while chasing hostiles deep in Mexico; he was killed by Mexican irregulars.

And there was Lieutenant Gatewood who was ignored by his superiors and treated so shabbily by our government, after the part he played in bringing Geronimo in. The modest, gentle Gatewood, after risking his life countless times against Apache hostiles, was injured in line of duty by an explosion while fighting a fire in a northern Army post. As a reward for years of service rendered, the gallant Gatewood was retired upon a lieutenant's pittance.

Lieutenant Almy was murdered by Apaches while on duty at San Carlos; the list could go on and on. There was Lt. Royal S. Whitman, of the "good heart," whose name is still under a cloud. He was hated and accused of crooked dealings by citizens of the Territory after he allowed Eskiminzin and his ragged, half-starved band of Aravaipas to come in and live near Old Camp Grant. Lieutenant Whitman was court-martialed for drunkenness, yet nowhere in his court-martial was he accused of crooked dealings. And no officer, not even excepting General Crook, was more respected and loved by Apaches he befriended.

The battles, running fights and skirmishes between the soldiers and

Apaches fill many volumes. But Corporal Hanlon was the first man over the wall in that bloody fight at the caves where the Apaches, singing their death-song, fought until they died.

Where Chaffee led the fight at Chevlon's Fork, that is better known as the Battle of the Big Dry Wash, all is peaceful and quiet today. The last time I was there, the only sounds I heard were the rustle of the wind in the pines and the drumming of a woodpecker.

Sgt. Reuben Bernard was court-martialed by Lieutenant Bascom after the tragic affair at Apache Pass in 1861, when the sergeant was insistent that Lieutenant Bascom exchange prisoners with Cochise. Had the lieutenant listened to the sergeant's entreaties, it might have avoided a long and bloody war. Lieutenant Bascom joined the Confederacy and did not survive the War Between the States. Sergeant Bernard rose from the ranks to a commission and finally won his star.

Of the many scouts who rose to fame, Al Sieber was, probably, best known. Sieber was with his Apaches, too, when he met his tragic end, a survivor of countless fights with Apaches. At the time of his death, Sieber was foreman over the Apaches when the road known today as the Apache Trail was being built. Sieber and his Indians were trying to dislodge a great boulder. The old scout saw it give. Sieber, crippled with old wounds, even then could have escaped. He waited to warn the Apaches, however, and the lion-hearted Sieber was crushed to death when the boulder crashed down on him.

Al Sieber, born in Germany, had fought in the Army of the North. Clay Beauford, another scout, had fought under General Lee. Born Bridwell, a Virginia boy, at fourteen he ran away from home and joined the Confederate Army. Brought home by his parents, he promptly ran away the second time, enlisting under the name of Clay Beauford. Twice wounded, he was with Pickett that fateful day at Gettysburg, and he survived that gallant, tragic charge.

And like so many of his kind, the West was in his blood. Enlisting as a private in the Fifth Cavalry in 1869, he rode with the "Dandy 5th." In Arizona he was discharged as a top sergeant in 1873. Serving for two years as a civilian packer and scout, it was as Captain of the San Carlos Apache Police, and later as Captain of Apache Scouts with a roving commission under the Territorial Governor, that Clay Beauford carved his name. Serving until 1880, he resigned to locate a ranch on the

Aravaipa and had his name legally changed to his real name, Bridwell—all because, as Bridwell said, he met "the girl with the long, yellow braids."

Croyden R. Cooley was another scout who made history in Arizona. The little town of Cooley was named for him until a lumber baron, years later, took it upon himself to have it changed to McNary. Yet Cooley is responsible for naming the little town of Showlow. Cooley and his partner fell out and agreed to play a game of Seven Up, the winner to take the great ranch. One point decided the game. "Show low," his partner said, "an' take the ranch." Cooley showed low and won it.

The famous scout was married to an Apache girl and many years ago one of Cooley's handsome sons, now dead himself, told me this incident: "My father, in charge of Apache scouts, had been sent into the Sierra Madres in Old Mexico after seven Apache renegades. He had just returned to Fort Apache, had taken his jacket off and was washing up when the C.O. sent for him; and without bothering to put his jacket on, he reported to the officer.

"Always on his return from Mexico he brought my mother presents, Mexican jewelry, any little thing he thought my mother would like. My mother saw the jacket on the peg and couldn't wait until father returned. She started going through its pockets; in one pocket was a little package that felt very soft to her touch. She knew it wasn't Mexican jewelry, but her curiosity finally got the best of her and mother opened the package. It contained seven human ears, proof my father brought back with him that the renegades were dead." The handsome Cooley laughed. "You know," he said, "that was the first and last time, too, mother ever let her curiosity get the best of her and went through my father's clothes."

One doesn't move far in Apache Land until stories come bobbing up. Cassadora Mesa and Cassadora Springs both bear the name of an old Apache chief. Because he was peaceful and friendly to the whites, his name is little known. Yet somehow I have never drank of the clear cold water but what the name of Captain Hamilton goes racing through my head.

Chief Cassadora and his peaceful little band were living on the reservation when some drunken Chiricahua Apaches killed two teamsters going into Fort Apache, and later boasted of the affair to other Indians. About seven hundred Apaches were located on the reservation at this

time. And it was Eskiminzin, chief of the Aravaipas, who called the council of the chiefs.

Fearing that the innocent would be punished with the guilty, that night when the moon was full all of the Apaches on the reservation— men, women and children—went streaming to the mountains. Nor was there any attempt to search out and punish the guilty parties. Troops were rushed into the field to pursue all fleeing Apaches, with orders to "take no prisoners."

Snow covered the high country. It was bitter cold in the hills. Bloody footprints in the snow made an easy trail to follow. Captain Hamilton and his troop were on the trail of Cassadora and his ragged little band. It was one evening at sundown an old squaw approached his camp. The captain, hearing the sentry's challenge, went himself to investigate. The old Apache woman was from Cassadora's band. They had harmed no one, she said; they were starving and freezing in the snow; Chief Cassadora wanted to come in and surrender his little band.

His orders were explicit, the captain said; he was to pursue the fleeing Apaches and take no prisoners. The old squaw went away.

Next morning at daybreak the captain was called again. Cassadora and his entire ragged, half-starved band were just outside his lines. To Captain Hamilton the chief spoke simply. He knew the captain's orders and he knew as a soldier the captain must obey. But rather than prolong their agony—they would soon starve and freeze to death—it would be much easier for him and his people to die by the bullets of the soldiers. Then the old chief and his entire band of men, women and children silently raised their hands above their heads and waited quietly for their end.

It was too much for the hard-bitten captain. To his everlasting credit, he disobeyed his orders. Captain Hamilton not only fed the ragged, half-starved band, he led them safely to San Carlos.

The officers, soldiers, the men of the line, the packers and the scouts, the bull whackers and mule skinners, stage drivers, prospectors and cow-punchers, the settlers and the Apaches, nearly all who rode and fought against this great backdrop of Apache Land are gone. Many died violent deaths and sleep in unmarked graves, yet all sleep quietly. And the eternal hills remain.

APACHE LAND TODAY

XX

THE APACHE who sat beside me on the top rail at the shipping pens removed his colored glasses and wiped them carefully, then with a pencil and notebook in hand he waited expectantly for the sale to begin. Cattle buyers from Texas, New Mexico, Colorado and Arizona roosted about us on the top rail, squatted on their heels or stood clustered in little groups inside the pen. A few figured with stub pencils as others hurled friendly insults at rivals across the big pen. The auctioneer tested his mike, made the usual wisecracks to the assembled buyers. Then the big gate was opened by an Apache cowboy, and the first bunch of steers was driven in.

It had been a dry winter, the cattle were thin after the gather and the long drive to the pens. But they were a good grade of range stock, they had been well classed, all were Herefords and uniform in size.

"You've already looked 'em over, boys," said the auctioneer. "Some of you have come a long ways. You know what's here for sale today, you know what you want. Make me an offer."

There was a slight pause, then a buyer on my right called, "Twelve." "Thirteen" called a buyer from across the pen, and the auctioneer launched into his sing-song: "Thirteen—thirteen—who'll give me the five? Five—five—five!" A nod from the first bidder. "Who'll give me the ten? Ten—ten—ten—who'll give me the fifteen?" As the bidding became spirited, the auctioneer's voice took on the staccato of machine-gun fire.

The first pen sold for $15.70 a hundred pounds. As fast as a pen was sold, the cattle were driven out and others were brought in. When one pen sold for $17.80 a hundred, I caught myself giving a low whistle, at which the Apache beside me removed his colored glasses and gave me a broad smile. They were Apache cattle and over a thousand head were sold that day.

An Indian stockman, an old white cowpuncher I had worked with years before, crawled up on the rail beside me. "Ever expect to see anything like this?" he said. I shook my head. "I don't know what this year's sales will reach, but last year, 1945, the Apaches sold almost a million dollars' worth of cattle on the San Carlos Reservation alone." My friend laughed. "Counting the beef the Apaches et on the roundup, it was a million dollars' worth of cattle that left the reservation."

As we walked over to the camp for chuck, some Apache cowboys rode in on good cow horses. They were half-Morgan and would look good in any remuda. The punchers' gear was good, too. My friend spoke with pride: "They've come a long ways since they used to ride them pistol-tailed ponies and pack off the guts from a white man's camp."

The change began in the early '20's. It took several years to gather all the white man's cattle. There had always been a few Apaches who owned cattle and, of course, there was the Tribal Herd. But now the whole reservation is their range. This does not mean that every Apache owns stock. There are many who do not own a cow. But each year cattle are issued to individuals from the Tribal Herd, a fine grade of Herefords, too, that is kept for breeding purposes. When twenty head of heifers is issued to an individual at cost, the Indian, if he keeps his nose clean, cannot help but prosper. When an Indian dies, his cattle are sold. The estate is divided among his family, and new allotments of cattle are issued. Many Apaches are becoming good cowmen.

There are some owning cattle, however, who won't even attend the roundup. They are fined five dollars a head for every one of their calves branded and usually seven-fifty for gathering one of their steers. The range is divided into various cattle associations and each association decides what fine they consider proper. White cowmen supervise, but more and more the operation of the range is going back to the Apaches themselves.

In the old days the agent was all powerful. He is still a potent factor but the Tribal Council wields tremendous power in administering the affairs of the reservation. It is evident in every way that the Apache is on his way up.

In the little town of Globe, only a few miles from the reservation, the Apaches have always been much in evidence. Today some of the Apache punchers dress much like Hollywood cowboys, without the artillery, of course; while their white brothers, in front of the Lodge saloon or across the street—depending on where the shade is—are dressed in more sombre hues. And to watch an Apache carry a sleeping child in his arms, with his wife at his side, empty-handed, is really something; in former times it was the woman who always carried the load.

They are regular attendants at the movies, too. A few years back I had gone to San Carlos to see an old Apache friend. Down on the reservation I was informed that he had driven to Phoenix with his family to see "Gone with the Wind," the round-trip calling for better than two hundred miles.

The married women still wear the colorful dress that was adopted in the '70's, but one seldom sees moccasins today; the shoes worn are flat-heeled and sensible. And it is not uncommon to see a daughter in bobby-sox at her mother's side, or dressed in a boy's shirt with the tail out and wearing levis rolled halfway to the knees.

Many attend the High School in Globe and they rate high scholastically. One Apache boy, back from the Navy, was asked the meaning of democracy. He couldn't answer. The instructor suggested: "Of the people, by the people, and for the people." He questioned the Apache boy again next day. "Of the people, by the people, and for the people," repeated the Apache. "Can you tell us anything more about democracy?" asked the instructor. "That's all I know," said the Apache. "I just got out of the Navy. I didn't learn anything about democracy there."

As a ward of the government, the Apache has no vote; yet he was subject to the draft. Many Apache boys have fine war records and there are some, like their white comrades-in-arms, who find it hard to readjust themselves to civil life.

Henry is an ex-marine with a fine service record; before he went into service he was a good cowboy, always dependable. He had come to the stockman's home that morning for some final instructions before going back on the mountain as a cowboy. He was tall for an Apache, six feet and slender. He was still in uniform and he wore it with pride. He was proud to be back, too. He had been hit on a beach-head in the South Pacific and there had been months in hospitals, but he was all right now. It would be good to be on a horse again, he had waited a long time.

Months later when I asked my friend Shorty, the stockman, about him, he shook his head. "He didn't stay long," he said. "He's in an' out of the guardhouse; gets drunk an' fights. Won't stay in camp alone. The war did something to Henry." Then, as an afterthought, my friend added: "Whether we know it or not, I guess the war did something to all of us, too."

"I remember the day he left," said Shorty. " 'I'd like to see you,' says Henry.

" 'What about?'

" 'I just want to see you,' he said.

" 'All right,' I says; an' according to Apache custom we sat a long time. Then he pulled a card from his pocket and handed it to me without a word. It was Henry's notice to report.

" 'You're not afraid?' I said.

" 'No,' said Henry. 'Not afraid, but me not come back.'

" 'What makes you think so?'

"He shook his head. 'Course, I kill some Japs first,' said Henry, 'but me not come back.'

"We shook hands an' more than the other Apache boys who left I hated to see him go. Then months later he came back for his leave before he went over, and hunted me up. I hardly knew him. We shook hands. 'Not afraid any more,' says Henry. I didn't get it and when Henry pointed to a little badge on his blouse I still didn't get it until he explained what it was. It meant that Henry was a fine shot with a rifle, an' was he proud of that little badge! Then it all came to me.

"One night in camp when we were killing a beef I gave Henry my six-shooter. There were six shells in the gun, too, not five. Henry wasn't six feet from the critter's head, either. He missed all six shots as he jerked the trigger instead of squeezing it off. We finally killed the beef with an axe. That was what was bothering Henry. He thought he was going to fight Japs with a six-shooter. No wonder it had Henry worried."

Many of the Apaches live in little houses now, and no matter how small the house, the idea seems to be to cut it into as many rooms as possible. Some have electric lights and refrigerators; everywhere the sewing machine is in evidence. But many Apaches still prefer the wickiup as a dwelling.

Our beneficent government never does things by halves. During the '30's, they built a toilet that was standard. They are everywhere on the San Carlos Reservation. Even then it was amusing to see one behind a brush wickiup. Today one finds these sentry boxes, built according to government specifications, standing in lonely grandeur on the big flats, although the wickiup has long since been abandoned.

Back in the 'teens, the government had a kind of makeshift housing project, the Apaches paying half the cost of the shack. These frame shacks were used as storage, for the most part, as the Apache preferred his tepee. When one of the washes came down, it cut into the bank and was about to wash a shack away; the owner got busy, pronto. He promptly sawed the shack in two, saving half; after which he reported and told the agent his half, the government's, had gone down the wash in the flood.

Since the Apache is still a ward of the government, any serious crime goes before the United States Commissioner and the offender is tried in Federal court. But on the Reservation itself, law infractions are dealt with by an Apache court and Apache judges. Apache police patrol the reservation; all of their offices are political.

It is the family groups that have crystallized into the various cattle associations, some of whose head men form the present Tribal Council. The adoption of the constitution and the Reorganization Act of 1934 brought no radical change.

When the depression came, many Apaches who worked off the reservation were forced to return. A construction program was instituted by the government: roads were built, water was developed, and the Apaches soon became apt with the machinery of road construction. It was not without its amusing incidents and always the Apaches' sense of humor was in evidence.

The local hoosgow at San Carlos was emptied—they were all minor offenders; a work camp was established for them on the mountain. Since they had their own cook and were well fed, no guard was needed. Nor did they slip any joints in a frenzy of labor. At the turn-off to their camp the prisoners made a dummy figure of an Apache. The clothes were stuffed with straw and a broomstick pointed to the camp itself. A little farther down the road they had painted on canvas in enormous letters the words "Sing Sing"; at the entrance to the camp they had erected a still larger sign: "Drive Slowly, Children at Play."

The Apache police were first organized by Agent John P. Clum, in 1874. By white punchers they were always known as the long-haired police. The police functioned well among their own people and it was only on rare occasions that the punchers and Apache police became involved.

Many years ago an old cowpuncher friend built a shack on the water inside the reservation line. The shack was only temporary, as the puncher knew that he was working against time. My friend's honesty may have been questioned but not his ambition or industry. Since he rode both early and late with a long rope and a running iron, it was not long until his brand was worn by considerable livestock that was, originally, not his own.

The agent at San Carlos, learning of the puncher's activities, sent word for him to get off the reservation and stay off! My friend's wife was sick. He sent word to the agent to that effect, saying he would leave as soon as his wife could travel. The agent, however, was "fed up," and no wonder! He sent twelve Apache police to the puncher's shack and they escorted the puncher to the agency at San Carlos.

My friend had not a leg to stand on. But when the agent, an ex-Army officer, insisted that my friend remove his hat and stand before him with bared head, hat in hand, he made a serious blunder. My friend, whose boiling-point was always low, resorted to violence. The agent missed the real fight that followed. The puncher flattened him with one punch; then the twelve long-haired police piled in and the real battle started. The puncher was finally subdued but it took all twelve police to do it.

Later, one of the Apache police, who lost a piece of an ear during the fracas, spoke in admiration of the fight my friend had made. "Twelve men," said the Apache, counting on his fingers; "twelve men, this cowboy he almost whip it."

Soldiers were stationed at Fort Apache on the upper reservation as late as 1923. Nor was there any love lost between most cowboys and the soldiers. In this respect the Apaches and the punchers stood on common ground.

Bob Anderson rode into our camp one evening to spend the night on his way to his asbestos claims. Bob was always quiet, but all the punchers cocked an ear whenever he spoke. "What about the time you stood off the United States Army?" the Old Man asked. "I never stood off no army," said Bob. "It was just a story that got around."

"I was running some horses on the reservation and the agent sent word to me to take the ponies off. I sent the agent word that I'd take 'em off just as soon as I got them gathered. I meant it, too. But the agent he got uppity and instead of sending his long-haired police he sent a lieutenant and a troop of cavalry to put me off the reservation.

"It was just a happen-so I saw them coming, so I crawled into the malapais above the trail. The shavetail was in the lead; when he got directly below me I throwed down on him with my Winchester and asked him what he wanted.

" 'I'm lookin' for one Robert Anderson with orders from the agent to put him off the reservation.'

" 'You're lookin' at him right now,' I says. 'Robert Anderson is my name,' and then I told this shavetail I was gathering my horses an' would get them off as soon as possible, but if he wanted trouble he could start his war right now. Since I was talkin' over the barrel of a .30-40, he got the point. He was all right, the shavetail was, an' plenty smart. He laughed and turned his troop around an' headed back down the trail. But about me standin' off an army, I wouldn't think of such a thing. It was just a story that got around. The shavetail was the only officer there, he only had one troop of cavalry."

In 1917, the 17th Cavalry was stationed in Globe for a period during the copper strike. They had hiked down on the reservation to exercise their horses. Both the Bar F Bar and the Cross S outfits were shipping cattle at Cutter that day. The soldiers had some led horses along. They were watering out and changing horses when a bunch of us rode over for a closer look at their horses.

"Don't go over there unless you want trouble," said an old waddie who was raised in Montana. "We're not lookin' for trouble," said a puncher, "just want to look at the ponies." "O.K.," said the old waddie, "but you're askin' for it."

When we rode up we exchanged friendly greetings. We were looking their horses over when a young trooper pointed to one of our stock saddles; it was a good one, too, made to order. "I rode one of them things once," he said. "I rode it for thirty miles an' it damn near killed me." "Chances are, that was the best ride you ever had," drawled a puncher; "but you bein' a soldier you wouldn't know it." From this point on, the tension began to grow.

When they changed horses, one of the troopers was bucked off. It didn't help matters any, of course, when the punchers laughed. The trooper was hurt; he was ashen in color when he mounted a second time, and was promptly thrown again. "Bet twenty dollars any man in the outfit can ride that thing," said a puncher, "an' that goes for Old Slick an' Greasy, the cook, too.' Just then a lieutenant appeared and broke it up. It was just as well he did, too, for anyone with half an eye could see trouble in the offing.

"What did I tell ya?" said the old Montana waddie as we rode back. "I've got nothin' personal against a soldier, but leave 'em where you find 'em or it's trouble sure. I mind one time, years ago, it was early morning. Our horses was at the rack, the outfit had gone into the saloon for a final snort before we went back to camp. Two soldiers set alone at a card table in the rear. Chances, they'd been there all night. But they were singing 'The Rolling River,' a song sung by the 7th Cavalry, Custer's old outfit. Even as a kid I'd always liked that song. So I took a full quart an' went back to give them a drink.

" 'Let 'em alone,' said the foreman, 'unless you're huntin' trouble.'

" 'I aint lookin' for trouble,' I says. 'I like that song an' just want to buy 'em a drink.'

" 'O.K.,' says the foreman, 'you're askin' for it.'

"The soldiers sung the song several times. We had several drinks. I remember singin' myself, but to this day I don't know how the fight started. But I must of been on the receiving end; it was two days before I could see well enough to tell a horse from a cow."

With the mining town of Globe only a few miles off the reservation and the coming of the railroad through the reservation, it is only natural that the San Carlos Apaches have been more influenced by the whites. Whether the influence has been for good or bad is still open to conjecture.

With the automobile and good roads, the White Mountain Apache has many contacts with the whites, but he is more remote, and the White Mountain Apaches on the upper reservation got a better deal in the first place when the reservation was laid out. At San Carlos there was only one year-round stream for irrigation, with less than one thousand arable acres. On the upper reservation there are six thousand acres of tillable land and the gurgle of the water from the irrigation ditches is as much a part of the reservation as the cedar, the piñons, the red earth and the blue sky overhead.

On both reservations Apache boys play basketball, soft ball, and hard ball. He plays with a rope now instead of a bow and arrows. He ropes dogs, chickens, his brothers and sisters, much as white ranchers' children do. And the three-day Rodeo has come to be almost as much a part of a coming-out party as the dances themselves.

The time in the roping isn't fast but there is an informality about it and fun, that has long ceased to exist among white punchers who follow the Rodeo as a business affair, where split seconds mean the difference in money won and lost. Riding under Rodeo rules, I doubt if there is an Apache rider on either reservation who could qualify in the bronc-riding at a big time Rodeo. But I'd rather watch an all-Apache Rodeo than the one at Madison Square Garden. As I said before, the Apaches are always good gamblers and, win or lose, they can always laugh.

"Chester A. Arthur coming out of shute number two," calls the Apache announcer. "Oliver Cromwell coming out of shute number four." Oliver Cromwell has no more than dusted his pants when another shute-gate opens. It is not surprising to see three shute-gates open at once—a pitching horse, a bucking bull, and a bucking steer all in a wild melee, to the amusement of all the Apache spectators.

In 1946 we went to an all-Indian three-day Rodeo at Fort Apache. There was a loud speaker for the Apache announcer and the booth itself was decorated with red, white and blue bunting and American flags. Apaches in wagons, trucks, and on horseback had come in to camp for the three-day affair. It was raining in the higher country but at least three inches of red dust lay over the Rodeo grounds.

The shute opened and a calf came out; as the flag dropped, out came the roper, going over and under as he poured it on the pony with the double of his rope. Nor was the rider alone, Indian dogs of all sizes went in pursuit and the whole outfit—calf, rider and Apache dogs—disappeared in a cloud of red dust to the amusement of the Indians.

The first day, four calves were turned out before a catch was made.

The second day, six calves left the shute before an Apache cowboy caught one. After the calf-roping, the team-tieing began, to be interrupted by a ball game between the Apaches and a colored team from McNary. It wasn't big league baseball, either, but Babe Ruth would have been proud of the two blows the big colored boy from the lumber camp at McNary struck.

After the ball game, the roping, the calf-tieing and the team-tieing started all over again and lasted until dark. The best catch made during the three days was when an Apache cowboy roped a flying Apache pooch that was in pursuit of his calf; over the loud speaker the Apache announcer called, "First money."

Two debutantes were "coming out" and there were three nights of dancing—the social dance, the Apache devil dance, in all its color and pageantry. And once again I slept through the final ceremony at sunrise.

Guy Sisson, an old friend, has lived and worked on both the upper and lower reservations for over twenty-five years. When a horse fell, tearing the ligaments in his right shoulder, it ended his days as a cowpuncher. Now he runs a garage at Fort Apache. He was always mechanically

inclined; even in the good old days, when we worked together, he looked out for hapless friends in the outfit. When I found a new cinch on my saddle, I had a good idea where it came from but, upon inquiry, Guy informed me curtly—"You'd a broke your damn neck if you tied onto anything big with that outfit."

My friend is dubious about the young Apache today while his warm eyes crinkle when he speaks of the old Apaches who have been his friends over the years, of their honesty and integrity.

When Sergeant Charles Bones, one of the old Apache scouts, was discharged at Fort Huachuca and came back to Fort Apache to live, he brought not only a good saddle horse but a good team and wagon as well. The old scout and the old cowpuncher soon became fast friends and the sergeant's manner of exercising his horses always interested the cowpuncher.

Instead of driving his team and leading his saddle horse behind the wagon Sergeant Bones simply worked it in reverse; he always rode the saddle horse while the team and wagon followed, followed him every place he rode. And my friend was curious, too, as to why the sergeant always found it necessary to exercise the wagon as well as the horses but he never asked the sergeant.

Time hung heavy on the sergeant's hands; aside from exercising the team and wagon he had nothing else to do, so Sergeant Bones opened a little restaurant in the Indian village called Canyon Day. My friend made out the purchase orders for the sergeant. Sergeant Bones' pension check usually came about the first of the month and it was a sizable order, too; along towards the end of the month, however, the orders were puny indeed. Since Sergeant Bones charged two bits a meal and served a generous helping to all who came, many Apaches found it much cheaper to eat with him and far more convenient. There were some months when the sergeant was hard put to break even.

In the old days, when an Apache died the wickiup and the deceased's possessions were burned. The owner's best horse was killed at the grave for he should be mounted well for his long journey through the land of shadows. Food was placed at the grave for the journey, too, and often a little corn for making tulapai, a favorite drink. The grave itself might be simply a crevice in the rocks, or a tree. Thirty years ago at the San Carlos Reservation the body of an old Apache who loved to watch the passing trains was buried beside the tracks, in the R.R. right-of-way.

Today the body is interred and since the killing of the horse at the grave is frowned upon by the authorities, the horse is often led up a remote canyon and killed, unbeknown to the authorities. The wickiup and the deceased's possessions are still burned. If the family is living in a house and a death occurs, the family moves out for several months.

Times change but old customs still persist. At the death of a squaw, a sewing machine is often placed on her grave; and canned goods, in great favor among the Apaches, are frequently placed at the grave for the long journey instead of former foods. Shortly after Prohibition was repealed, a cowpuncher riding onto an Apache grave found, instead of the corn for making tulapai, six quart bottles of a well-known brand of beer.

Today approximately six thousand Apaches, about equally divided, live on both reservations and, as with their white brothers and sisters, there are all kinds of Apaches, too. No land can be sold on the reservation but improvements may be, and many Apaches have proven themselves sharp traders. Others are desperately poor. There are some who are in regular attendance at the white man's church, while others are constantly in the guard house.

Many own modern trucks and good cars. Individual steer checks often run into thousands of dollars. Instead of the pony beside the wickiup, one often sees one of General Motors' best products; and, like their white brothers, there are many who seem to specialize in old wrecks and a yard-full of junk.

Yet the medicine man still functions. Apache debutantes have their coming-out parties, when the sacred pollen is sprinkled on all attendants the final morning with the coming of the rising sun. Through it all is the color and pageantry of their ceremonies.

Cars driven by Apaches and whites either streak or rattle along the main highways that lead through the reservation but on the reservation, itself, the horse is still king. And if one rides a pony on a moonlit night he will find tepees, ghostly in the moonlight; above the slow, steady beat of drums he will hear an Apache voice in song, rising and falling in cadence, not unlike that of the singer's brother, the coyote. For it is still Apache Land.